1846 BEFORE & AFTER

HISTORICAL GUIDE TO THE ANCIENT PARISH OF BURY

1846—Before and After

An Historical Guide to the

Ancient Parish of Bury

by

The Reverend ARTHUR J. DOBB, D.A.(Manc.)

Vicar of Bircle

with a foreword by

The Reverend J. REGINALD SMITH, M.A.

The Rector of Bury

08556389

4000152986

01900279

Published by
BIRCLE PARISH CHURCH COUNCIL
1970

Printed by
BURY TIMES LIMITED
Cross Street Bury Lancashire

Cover designed by ,
The Author

Bury 1848. From an oil painting by James Sharples showing the Parish Church amidst the factory chimneys. St. Marie's can be seen far right.

FORWARD BY THE RECTOR OF BURY

"Yea, we have a goodly heritage".

It is a good thing for all of us to be reminded from time to time of the effort and foresight, the sacrifice and vision, which have gone into the building up of our home-land or township.

Those who take the trouble to state clearly for us what is known or can be surmised about the history and growth of our town are in one sense historians, in another sense prophets, for they not only recall but open our eyes to the fact that history has been made here and that we are making history today.

That the story of Bury is an interesting one none can deny, and that the church in Bury has had a vital part to play in the forming of that story is very clear to those who read what is written in this book. It is a great privilege to be associated with the Author in this, the second of his written treasures about life and work here in Bury.

I pen these words on the Eve of the Feast of St. Peter. "Thou art Peter, and on this Rock I will build my Church".

Set on the Rock, the centre of this long established town, with its spire pointing our eyes heavenwards, the Parish Church is a constant reminder that our forebears set God ever before them, central in life and work.

What there is to be ashamed of in our history we will not repeat, what there is to inspire us we will be thankful for, and return thanks by building an even greater heritage for the future.

ACKNOWLEDGMENTS

My grateful thanks are due to many residents in Bury both for their help and encouragement in the compilation of this book.

Especially I would express my gratitude to the owners of the ancient halls who have allowed me to visit their homes and take the photographs : Mr. and Mrs. G. L. Wilde of Hey House, Mr. and Mrs. G. Baldwin of Lumb Hall, Mr. and Mrs. Taylor of Brandlesholme Old Hall and Mrs. M. Hutchinson of Lower Chesham Hall.

To the Rev. J. R. Smith, Rector of Bury, and the clergy who have so readily provided information about their Church and Parish. The Rev. D. Gray Vicar of All Saints', Elton: the Rev. J. D. Driver, Rector of Holcombe: the Rev. H. W. Marcroft, Vicar of Edenfield: The Rev. A. Hulse, Vicar of St. John's, Bury, The Rev. M. T. E. Hagarty, Vicar of Walmersley : The Rev. M. Hunt, Vicar of Walshaw and the Rev. J. McClelland, Minister of Bank Street Chapel.

Also to the many people in industry who have given of their time. Mr. J. C. Kenyon of Jas. Kenyon & Son Ltd. : Mr. H. Webb of Joseph Webb & Sons Ltd. : The Personnel Manager of Joshua Hoyle & Sons (Bacup) Ltd. : The Secretary of Bury Trustee Savings Bank : The Secretaries of the Rochdale Equitable Pioneers' Society Ltd. and the Bury District Co-operative Society Ltd.

I am indebted to Mr. Robson and Mr. Asquith, the Headmaster and the Deputy of Bury Grammar School for Boys, to Mr. Petts, Headmaster of Bury Church School and to Mrs. C. Holt for the loan of her thesis "A History of a School". Also to Miss Christine Waters for her project on "The Cotton Industry of Heywood" : Chief Inspector Greenwood of Bury (N) Division for information on the Lancashire Constabulary : The Tramway Museum Society : Mr. R. S. Greenwood of the Roach Valley Railway Society and to the Rev. R. Carmylie for help in industrial research.

Assistance has been readily given by members of the Bury Town Clerk's Department : the Curator of Bolton Museum : the Librarian and Staff of both the Bury and Heywood Libraries and the Curator of the Castle Museum at York.

Finally my thanks to Mr. and Mrs. F. Heywood for checking the script : to my colleague Captain J. Etheridge of the Church Army for his work on the photographs and to my wife who has undertaken typing the manuscript in readiness for the printer.

INTRODUCTION

Every Lord's Day millions of English Christian men, women and children worship the Lord God through faith in the Lord Jesus Christ. As the people of God in any locality, be it city, town or country village, they gather in their Parish Church, or Non-Conformist Chapel as previous generations have done before them. One such congregation was reminded of their spiritual duties by two cards fixed to the main door. As you walked into Church the notice read "Come in and worship with us" whilst on leaving the Christians read "Go out and witness for us." Each member then has a particular duty and task to fulfill in their own Church and in the area where they live at just one point in the span of time.

There are moments which are especially remembered by those faithful People of God. Jesus told His Disciples as He instituted the Lord's Supper "Do this in remembrance of me" and since that time the Lord's Death, which the Bible alludes to as the "Climax of history", has been recalled on the first day of each week in the Lord's Supper or Holy Communion Service. Other events are remembered each year as a birthday whilst for others it may be "every Preston Guild" or century. In 1971 we celebrate the 125th Anniversary of the Consecration of Bircle Parish Church. There are many Churches older, many finer pieces of architecture and others which may mean more to you, my Reader, but to the Parishioners of Bircle the Church is their Church. In it many of their parents and grand-parents before them have come to offer worship and thanksgiving to God as well as seeking His goodness upon their Marriage or His strength and comfort in their sorrow.

The purpose of this book is to try and get a glimpse of life for the first congregation of Bircle Church and does not pretend to be a history. In 1846 Queen Victoria had been on the throne of England for just nine years, the stage coaches rumbled along ill-kept and unguarded roads, the "penny" post was still in its infancy whilst cars, radios and even sewing machines were still things of the future. In the sphere of literature Charles Dickens was immortalising the times with his pen portraits of many characters like Oliver Twist. It was still another forty years before the escapades of Sherlock Holmes at 23A Baker Street were created. In music the works of Beethoven were becoming better known, it was the year when Mendelssohn completed his "Elijah" whilst such frivolities as the Savoy Operas of Gilbert and Sullivan or the serious meditations of Stainer's "Crucifixion" were still a generation away.

The entry headed "Bircle" in Nikolaus Pevsner's book "Buildings of England, South Lancashire" simply records "St. John Baptist. On the hillside, up Castle Hill. Nave with bellcote and chancel. By G. Shaw of Saddleworth 1845. A Commissioners Church (cost £1,350 only). Fine view of mills and chimneys". On the 1st July 1846 the Bishop of Chester consecrated the Church and it still stands on the hillside but rather more homely than the barren edifice graced by his lordship a century and a quarter ago.

Bircle Church

Since the 1st July, 1846, much has happened, events for better or for worse have shaped the affairs of men and I have sought to outline some of these to try and grasp an idea of the lot of those who perhaps watched the Church built and cared for it in those early days. Every Church has a similar tale and I trust that through these pages you will be thankful to God for your own life in 1971, for the Church which He has provided for you wherever that may be and I pray that they may be a means of realising the debt to those who have gone before us which can be paid in part to those who shall follow.

CONTENTS

CHAPTER 1 — A SEARCH FOR 1846

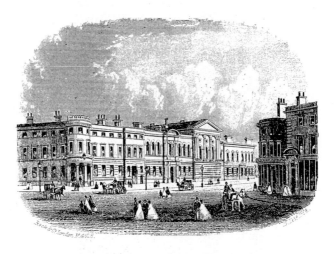

The Market Place in 1864 looking towards Market Street, The Derby Hotel, old Town Hall and Athenaeum.

1846 — an inconspicuous date amid the early years of the industrial revolution. Many of the farm homesteads of the moorlands beyond Bury had already been standing for over 100 years giving shelter to the sparse and rugged population. The task to find life 125 years ago has peculiar problems in Bury since succeeding generations have preserved little of their heritage.

Standing in the "Market Place" for the first time one gets the impression that the nameplate has strayed away from home. There is the Parish Church once misguidedly described by a Bishop of Manchester as "the gem of the Diocese", in the centre of the triangular place is a statue of Sir Robert Peel, Bury's famous statesman, whilst facing the Church spire is a mixed facade left over from Victorian prosperity. Towards the back of this "Market Place" are two more promising buildings. A three-storey Georgian brick house with a fine doorway looks across to the painted half-timbered front of the "Two Tubs". These last two buildings were certainly there in 1846 — but what else? Looking around the Market Place it is difficult to realise to-day that the site had been an important centre of a widespread woollen trade which was once England's great industry. Over the years the active centre in Bury has gradually moved away from the Market Place except for the complex road junction and by the end of 1971, with the northerly bye-pass this hive of traffic will be much quieter.

The Georgian doorway, Bury Market Place : date late 18th cent.

Bury ! What's in the name ? It is said to be a word of Saxon origin meaning a stronghold although which way of spelling it seems to have caused some problems. Other renderings, besides the one with which we are familiar are Biri (1194) : Buri (1212) : Byry (1292) and Bery (1323). Before the River Irwell was diverted into its present course it flowed by the foot of the rock which provided the platform for the fortified Manor house, Parish Church and a few houses nestling round the village square. There has been an easy crossing of the Irwell at some point below "Castlecroft" since early days and this precious ford needed the "stronghold's" protection. A small hamlet was certainly on the rock before "1066 and all that" but any description would be a product of imagination. In Bury's Museum is one link with the town's early beginnings — a Roman Urn containing a considerable number of small bronze coins dated between A.D. 253-282. These were found two or three miles north of the centre and there is no evidence of Bury being of any significance to the Roman invaders.

Fortunately Julius Caesar, who led the first Roman invasion in 55 B.C., was in the habit of keeping a diary. From these memoirs and other early writers we get a picture of England in those far off days. The land was covered with huge forests interspersed with marshes and the wild life such as deer, wolves, boar, bears and badgers roamed freely amongst them. What communities there were consisted of small groups of round thatched wooden dwellings from which the early

Britons hunted the game. These small outcrops of primitive village life were linked by tracks through the undergrowth and across the treacherous marshy areas. It was the Roman Lieutenant Agricola who became the architect of transforming, by British labour, the Celtic meandering paths into the straight metalled roads like the one which ran from Manchester to Ribchester via Radcliffe and Affetside. Minor roads were added to the network to link strategic crossing of rivers or vantage points. Our knowledge of Britain during the latter years of the Roman occupation is very scanty and Bury's historic hoard comes from those mystic days — perhaps coins jettisoned by a fleeing garrison as it made a hasty retreat from a band of marauders who ravished the land.

After King William I and his Norman knights had divided England up as their loot a survey of estates and Churches was ordered by the Monarch. This ancient census has become famous through its title — Domesday Book and is dated 1086. Some writers maintain that this ancient record states that Roger de Poictou is the Patron of Bury Parish Church whilst others totally reject the idea that Bury is even mentioned in the Domesday Book. (See Appendix). Whatever the truth it is certain that the estates and patronage of Bury changed hands a number of times before the long dynasty of the Stanley family, whose title is the Lords of Derby. It is unlikely de Poictou ever saw Bury as the manor was one knight's fee and in 1193 the tenant bore the local name of Adam de Bury. A family called Lacy were next to own Bury as part of their holdings which also included the Manor of Tottington and it was during their regime that the latter passed into the ownership of the crown and has been known ever since as the "Royal Manor of Tottington".

The next name on the history books is Pylkington and it is known that one of this family, a John de Pylkington was Rector of the Parish in 1386. Their fortunes lasted for about a hundred years when disaster struck through the War of the Roses. The struggle for power lasted about thirty years and came to a sudden end with the battle at Bosworth in 1485. The opposing forces were the House of York and the claims of Richard III who had the support of the Pylkingtons and the House of Lancaster in the personage of the Duke of Richmond. At Bosworth events took place which were to destine the future of England and Bury. Richard was killed, Thomas Pylkington captured and later executed and the Duke of Richmond was crowned on the battle-field as King Henry VII by Sir William Stanley. To reward the Stanleys for their loyalty to the new King during the struggle for power, Thomas, Lord Stanley was created Lord of Derby and the lands of Bury confiscated from the Pylkingtons and duly presented to him. Life, however, was never secure in the Middle Ages but subject to the whims and fancies of the Monarchs. Although Lord Stanley had played such an active part in helping the Tudors overcome Richard and other claimants to the throne his favour ran out and he himself was finally executed by Henry. The Pylkingtons must have feared the worst much earlier than events took place for in 1465 they obtained a License to fortify the Manor House and it was this building with its adaptations which became known as the Castle for there is no evidence of any major fortress in the town.

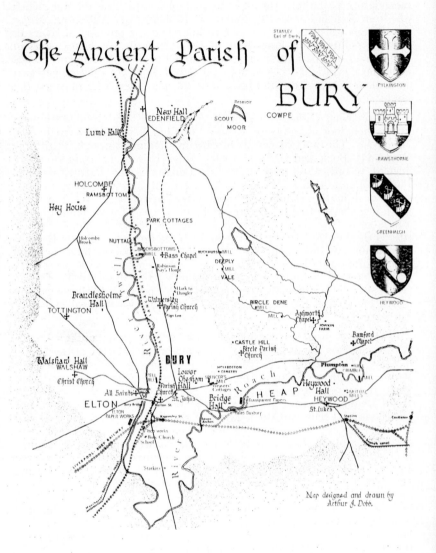

The Ancient Parish of BURY

PYLKINGTON

RAWSTHORNE

GREENHALGH

HEYWOOD

STANLEY
Earl of Derby

COWPE

Resevoir

New Hall
EDENFIELD

SCOUT
MOOR

Lumb Hall

HOLCOMBE
RAMSBOTTOM

Hey House

PARK COTTAGES

Holcombe
Brook

NUTTAL

BROOKSBOTTOMS
MILL

Bass Chapel

BUCKHURST
MILL

DEEPLY
MILL
VALE

Robinson
Kay's House

Lark to
Dangler

Brandlesholme
Hall

TOTTINGTON

Walmersley
Parish Church

BIRCLE DENE
MILL

MILL

Ashworth
Chapel

IOWKIN
FARM

Bamford
Chapel

CASTLE HILL
Bircle Parish
Church

Walshaw Hall
WALSHAW

Christ Church

BURY

Lower
Chesham
Hall

HOLKBOTTOM
CEMETERY

SPENCER'S
MILL

Weavers
Cottages

Plumpton

CRIMBLE
MILL

Heywood
Hall
HEYWOOD

MELTHAM
MILL

All Saints
Parish Church

St. John's

Bridge
Hall

Transparent Papers

ELTON

ELTON
PAPER WORKS

Bolton St.

Knowsley St.

Seven
Arches

Yates Duxbury

St. Lukes

Station

Castleton

Bury Bridge

Dye Works

School

Bast Church

Starkies

LIVERPOOL BURY RAILWAY

River Roach

Rochdale canal

Map designed and drawn by
Arthur J. Dobb.

The Earls of Derby governed their manor, mainly by proxy, from the fortified Manor house which stood between Bolton Street and the Drill Hall. What local government existed came from the court-leet presided over by the Lord of the Manor. The annual feature was the appointment of three constables who endeavoured to give some sort of law enforcement. Nothing remains to recount the events save some coins from the reigns of the Edwards : Henry VIII : Elizabeth I and the Stuarts. One fact of lasting importance emerges from the reign of Edward III (1327-1364). It is said that during this period emigrant Flemmings settled in Bury and "fabricated their webs from the fleeces grown in the forest of Tottington". Presumably those were the first beginnings of the woollen industry which is still in evidence in this town amidst the cotton belt of Lancashire. In 1440 the market was first established and our Market Place became the spot for meeting friends, conducting business and enjoying the hospitality of the numerous ale-houses. John Leland, librarian to king Henry VIII and a journeyman visited the market in about 1535 and seemed unimpressed ; he wrote "Byri on Irwel Water, 4 or Vmiles from Manchester, but a poore market" — hardly a fitting description for the present market ! It is elsewhere reported that the Manor House was one of the twelve Lancashire fortified Halls destroyed by the Parliamentary Troops in 1644, but Leland states "There is a ruine of a castel by the paroch chirch yn the towne".

From 1750 to 1846 many alterations took place in the administration of the growing township. The mediaeval court-leet with its indifference to improvement gave place to a Committee known as the "Select Vestries". The Rector, Churchwardens, Constables and any co-opted man of influence formed this august body. For nearly 100 years they endeavoured to match the demands of an exploding industrial town. The care of the poor and sick ; the need for road improvement ; provision of lighting and sanitation and so on became far and beyond the scope which could be reasonably expected from any small group of men acting in their spare time. On 27th July, 1846, an Act of Parliament called "The Bury Improvement Act" set up a new governing body, in place of the Select Vestry, and to be elected by the ratepayers. From the appointed date 27 Commissioners were to form the first town "Council" and each year nine had to be elected. Another Act in 1872 increased the number of Commissioners to thirty. Bury's first ever elections had taken place some fourteen years earlier when, in 1832, the town returned its first member of Parliament.

The year 1846, besides being the year a small country Chapelry was consecrated in Bircle, was the year the semi-feudel system which had grown out of the Mediaeval ways was sentenced to the history books. The two great land-lords in Bury, the Rector and Lord Derby, still held considerable influence in the town but as the years have passed the town has been governed by its Council duly elected by its inhabitants and the scene of our present pursuit transformed. Since the mid-nineteenth century much has happened which we will look at to see how much better is our lot than that of the early industralists and to consider how they looked forward with hope of better things. The story to 1846 must also have its place in our search. Men like John Kay and Robert Peel have a significant place, events like the canal, railway and tramway have done much to develop the town and services such as the Post Office and Schools have played their part.

APPENDIX — Domesday Book

The British Museum has furnished the following information regarding the opposing statements : "The section of Domesday Book relating to Lancashire (which was not included as a county in the Survey) has been translated and analysed in the "Victoria History of the Counties of England" . . . there is no reference to Bury in the Index to Domesday of Lancashire, neither is it marked on the accompanying map which shows the names of places, mentioned in the Survey.

However, in a Note to Domesday Map, the compiler William Farrer writes : "The sparcity of place names in South and East Lancashire was not entirely due to paucity of manors, but partly to the character of the Survey, which sometimes omits the names of manors or berewicks dependant upon capital manors. Thus Domesday enumerates . . . . 21 berewicks in Salford hundred . . . without recording their names".

Bury is not mentioned then in Domesday but it is reasonable to assume that Bury is one of the unnamed manors.

The Author's impression of Mediaeval Bury. Buildings from left to right are the Wool Inspector's shop (based on a shop in the York Castle Museum); the fortified Manor House; the half-timber houses and hostelries (based on a plan of Bury in 1815 and a model of Bolton Market Place); the Parish Church, typical of Lancashire's Gothic Churches as at Deane and Edenfield.

CHAPTER 2—FROM THE MARKET CROSS TO THE MILL

Like hundreds of other market towns Bury had its own Market Cross, and around that simple stone symbol the life of the common people was woven into a fabric of invention and ingenuity which helped Lancashire play such an important part in English history. The cross was erected in the days of Queen Elizabeth I and eventually fell to the ravages of time in 1818 when extensive alterations were made in the Market Place. The only decoration on the cross was the date and the arms of the de Bury family. It stood on a base of three steps suggesting the three graces spoken of by the Apostle Paul "Faith, Hope and Charity and the greatest of these is Charity".

When the town's folk first erected their cross the total population could have hardly exceeded six or seven hundred. It is stated that in 1377 there was no town in Lancashire with a greater population than eight hundred and village life and labour altered very little in the Mediaeval days. The town became important as a focus of the moorland woollen industry for in the reign of Elizabeth I a "Woolnager" or cloth inspector was appointed in Bury. His duties were to measure and certify the quality of woollen cloth and to collect the badly needed tax which was payable on each piece of cloth produced. The whole process from the natural wool to the finished garment was done in the isolated homesteads — it was a part of family life along with the farm, and what 'modernisation' there was normally meant one home concentrating on one of the processes. Weaving was reasonably quick but spinning was a real problem. Even with the use of the spinning wheel, a German invention of the 16th century, one loom could use the total thread output from four or five "spinsters".

Cotton goods began to arrive in the 17th century and the manufacture from the raw cotton fibres in the damp atmosphere of Lancashire about 1640. The spinning and weaving of cotton simply followed the pattern established by wool and so the new industry grew happily alongside the old. Sometimes the two were mixed to provide a lighter material. For almost one hundred years this way of life continued without much alteration then in 1704 a boy was born called John. He lived some four miles north of Bury in one of the farms in a hamlet called Park, overlooking Ramsbottom and the Irwell Valley. John, his Surname was Kay, was an ingenius lad and whilst apprenticed to a reed-maker for weaving looms he developed a flattened metal wire to replace a bulkier wooden strip to hold the "warp" threads. He is most famous for his "Flying Shuttle". Shuttles were in regular use in weaving but they had to be thrown across the loom by a weaver at each end of the "weft" (the cross threads). In 1733 John Kay designed a "picking stick" which caused the shuttle to fly across the loom which meant that the loom could be operated by just one man.

It might be thought that such inventions and improvements for the home-weavers would be welcome. The staple industries of Great Britain were at a very low ebb during the reign of Queen Anne and any help to the export market would be greeted with delight. This was far from the events. In a publication called "The New Library of

This Portrait of JOHN KAY, of Bury,

(Inventor of the Fly Shuttle &c.)

was saved, during the Earthquake that occurred on the Island of Juan Fernandez, and is dedicated to

The Right Hon:ble Sir Rob:t Peel Bart. M.P.

by his obedient, humble Servant,

Tho.s Sutcliffe

Proof
(Fat. Sea. Hall.)

"These inventions, like every other invention which has contributed to the extraordinary advance of the cotton manufacture, were opposed by the workmen, who feared that they would lose their employment; and such was the persecution and danger to which John Kay was exposed that he left his native country and went to reside in Paris.
So hard is the fate of inventors, when they fail, no one pities them; when they succeed, persecution, envy, and jealousy, are their reward. Their means are generally exhausted before their discoveries become productive. They plant a vineyard and either starve or are driven from their inheritance before they can gather the fruit. This melancholy truth is exemplified at every stage of the cotton manufacture, which is the creature of mechanical inventions."

Baines History of the County Palatine of Lancaster.

20

Park Cottages: Birthplace of John Kay

Useful Knowledge" it was reported that "At this time the demand (of yarn) exceeded the supply, and the weaver was continually pressing the spinner, which was further aggravated by the invention of the Fly Shuttle, in 1733 by Mr. John Kay of Bury, Lancashire". So much for the press reports but his treatment at the hands of his fellow workers was far worse. The mural in Manchester Town Hall depicts the hand-workers breaking into his home whilst John and his family flee for their lives. His home was broken up, the flying shuttle loom smashed and he finally settled in Colchester. John, however, did have a few friends who published a short document called "A testimonial in behalf of Merit neglected and genius unrewarded and record of the Services and Sufferings of one of England's greatest benefactors". The development of South East Lancashire as the great cotton manufacturing area of the world is in part the testimony to John Kay.

Soon the cotton industry was to take on a new look. John Kay is linked to Lower Chesham Hall by his autograph. The hall was built either in 1712 or 1719 by Richard Kay but has been disfigured by the addition of "St. Paul's Institute". The house is more typical of the 17th century than the 18th century and inside it has the atmosphere of a good honest home. The staircase is simple but fitting, well lit by its mullioned windows on the half-landings. Each window is divided into diamond shaped panes and on one of the panes is the signature "John Kay 1720" probably engraved with a diamond ring, a common piece of jewellery for the men of his day.

Lower Chesham Hall : built 1712

The Weavers' Cottages : Chesham Fold

The Ford Madox Brown Mural painting in Manchester Town Hall of John Kay and his family fleeing from the handweavers.

By permission of the Manchester Corporation.

Below Chesham Old Hall on Rochdale Old Road stands a row of Weavers' Cottages called Chesham Fold, which, at the time of writing has a demolition order on it. These cottages are the last remaining link in Bury between the home cotton industry and the mills which were to become so much a part of the Lancashire scene. They were built in 1783 as an industrial enterprise to provide a home for the cotton weaver and his family whilst the third floor was a workroom. This particular row is quite unique because they have a half-floor in the upper storey, no doubt used for the storing of the woven fabric. In some Weavers' Cottages the top floor was open across the whole terrace to provide a communal workroom, a valuable asset for machines like Crompton's Mule. The flying shuttle gave the opportunity for a man to work alone and it may well be that these cottages have some link with John Kay's son who invented the "drop box" in 1760 so that various colours could be used in the weft.

A note about Samuel Crompton will complete our story from the Market Cross to the Mill. He was born at Firwood, a small hamlet not six miles from Bury but nearer Bolton, in 1753. Early in his life the family moved about a quarter of a mile to a picturesque Tudor mansion called Hall i' th' Wood. After his fathers' death Samuel provided for his mother and sisters by farming and cotton spinning, using a "Spinning Jenny" a machine invented by James Hargreaves of Blackburn. The inefficiency of the Jenny exasperated Samuel and at the age of 21 he began a spare time struggle, which was to last five years, to provide a method which would produce fine quality yarn quickly and without the incessant breaks in the thread he experienced on the Jenny. He developed a machine wich incorporated principles of both the Jenny and Richard Arkwright's "Water Frame". The result was nicknamed the "Mule". The main features was being able to spin 12 cops at once, even if turning the large wheel by hand was exhausting. When the news of the Mule leaked out the industrial

23

Firwood : birthplace of Samuel Crompton

parasites descended. So unscrupulous were the spies that on one night he had to fight off a group at a bedroom window who had come equipped with ladders and torches to steal his ideas. The Mule was simple but effective and is one of the few survivors from the machine antagonists.

Crompton had burnt much mid-night oil and spent all his spare money to build the Mule, but this did not deter the greedy cotton manufacturers from industrial robbery. He was destitute and eventually agreed to exhibit his work for a guarantee of £60. The machine was shown, mercilessly copied and some of the exhibition sponsors refused to pay their share of his guarantee. Later a few friends came to the rescue and managed to obtain an award for him of £5,000. Crompton had the added satisfaction to see the Mule working in his spinning mill at Back King Street, Bolton, from 1802-1815. Although a man of great ability and industry with demands upon his time and

Crompton inventing spinning mule

By kind permission of Bolton Corporation.

funds he was for many years the regular organist at the Swedenborgist Church in Bolton and even built his own organ. He died in 1827 and was buried at the Parish Church in Bolton.

Once the inventions began to make their impression on the industry the home workers in Lancashire began to revolt because they feared their livelihood would be ruined. Many groups formed who marched into the cotton towns and ransacked any pretence of new machinery. In 1826 one such group was planning to march on Bury, the military were alerted and a watchman set on the roof of the "Crooked Billet" a three-storey hostelry in the Wylde which held a good view of Bury Bridge. About mid-day the watchman, not having seen any signs of movement all morning, went downstairs for his lunch. During his meal-break the workers came down from Brandlesholme, across Bury Bridge and had invaded many premises before the soldiers could afford any protection to either life or property. The risings were however short lived for the tide of machines was advancing and the workers had as much hope of deterring the financiers from building mills to house the new equipment as King Canute had of holding back the sea with a yard brush. The scene was very soon to change from fighting industrial-isation to trying to survive within it. It was only months away before the first cotton mills were in operation nestling down in the valleys of Lancashire where water power was easy to find, Birtle Dene and Deeply Vale.

Hall i'th' Wood : the birthplace of the spinning mule

Crompton's Spinning Mule
By kind permission of Bolton Corporation.

The Flying Shuttle and the Mule were the two inventions which were mainly responsible for the rise of the cotton mills. Other inventions were needed and they came along in due time but the two great names which shaped the future of Lancashire are John Kay and Samuel Crompton. The story from an industry centred around the Market Cross to the highly developed mechanised industry is their story which unfortunately reveals not just the ingenuity of a few men but the fear, greed and lusts of many others.

The ancient Parish Church of Bury as it is today

Photo: "Bury Times".

CHAPTER 3—TWO GEMS

The plot of land flanking the east side of the Market Place has been set aside for the worship of God from time immemorial. It is questionable whether the Celtic monks from Iona or Lindisfarne ever planted one of their crosses in the field and named it as the "kirk-feld" as happened in the neighbouring town of Bolton. A Church has been there for 1,000 years for the earliest tradition suggests that a House of God was first built in A.D. 971. This may well be true as it accords with the year in which Parishes were first formed in the reign of King Edgar. Another tradition says the beginnings were in 1290 or even as late as 1535 but both these are later than the first Rector, which would appear a strange sequence of events if they were true.

The area assigned as Bury Parish was extensive and varied in character : to the east of the town were the waste shrublands which flanked the River Roach whilst travelling north up the Irwell Valley high moorland country overlooks the narrow plains.

At least three Churches have stood on the site, the present one having been designed by J. S. Crowther reputed to be a copy of Tintern Abbey — if this is so it is a feeble attempt to imitate grace and elegance. There are no remains of the earlier buildings but the Church-warden accounts of 1743-1769 refer to improvements in the Church and the erection of an organ with a gallery at the West End. The introduction of such a musical instrument was by no means universally welcomed. The Puritan fathers of the 17th century had bitterly opposed such music. At the Restoration there were few men left in England who were capable of building an organ and it was the continental organ builders who brought the art back to this land. Also the Puritan teaching lingered in the hearts of many of their congregation who feared that introducing organs would destroy the sanctity of the House of God and His Worship.

The concerted efforts of the mid-eighteenth century congregations to preserve their Mediaeval building with its organ was of no avail. In 1776 a meeting presided over by the Hon. and Rev. J. Stanley resolved to demolish and rebuild the Church whilst retaining the Mediaeval tower and spire. The scheme was set in hand and duly completed. About 1842 the tower and spire, which stands to-day replaced the tower still standing from the Mediaeval Church. Crowther, the architect of the present Church, wrote that the "Georgian Church was rendered, if possible, still more unsightly by contrast with the purer work in the Revived Pointed style which was added later". Having derided the Georgian builders for their nave he turned his scorn to the steeple as "more suited in character and dimensions to a small village Church than to an important Parish Church in the centre of a large town". Crowther obviously felt able to convince the building committee that, at the worst, the height of the tower and spire would be increased, at the best it would be rebuilt. What he termed "the village steeple" was virtually ignored in his design for the new nave and chancel, so to try and provide for all eventualities he built a narthex between the existing tower and the over-high nave. Unfortunately

The Parish Church after the building of the 1842 spire and before rebuilding in 1876.

the two structures are out of proportion with each other and Crowther was even less successful than the Georgians whom he so readily criticised. Designs from other architects did not solve the problem but at least some did accept the tower and spire as a permanent feature.

During the four and a half years which the present Church took to build the Services were held in the Town Hall (now the Derby Hall). The 1780 Church was closed after a century of service and the present one opened in February, 1876. If you visit the ancient Parish Church you will find that the guide book written by the Very Rev. R. S. Wingfield-Digby and more recently revised by the present Rector, the Rev. J. R. Smith will fill in much of the story briefly mentioned in these notes.

A well known Lancashire historian, Canon Raines, compiled a list of the Rectors of Bury, mainly from the archives of the Episcopal Registers at Lichfield, which Diocese covered nearly the whole of Western England before the formation of the Chester Diocese in the reign of Henry VIII. This list begins "1187 Peter" and concludes "1966 John Reginald Smith". Between the two are thirty-six names of men who have served the Parish for periods ranging from forty years (the Rev. Sir Wm. Henry Clerke 1778-1818) to six years (the Rev. John Lightfoot 1654-1660). Perhaps just two of this long list of Divines could be mentioned for their contribution to our story.

30

THE HON^{ble} JOHN STANLEY, BROTHER OF 11 TH EARL OF DERBY

The only immediate member of the Stanley family to be instituted to the living of Bury was the Hon. and Rev. John Stanley, the younger brother of the eleventh Earl of Derby, who was Rector for 35 years from 1743-1778. In his day he must have been one of the wealthiest clerics this country has ever known. Along with the Parish of Bury he also held the livings of Liverpool and Halsall. His wealth was used

31

St. John's Chapel-of-Ease built in 1770. Exterior from The Rock.
By kind permission of Borough Librarian.

St. John's Chapel-of-Ease. Interior.
By kind permission of the Borough Librarian.

St. John's in the Rock

For centuries the Parish Church ministered to the spiritual needs of the town alone. It became obvious as the town expanded that sooner or later other "spiritual homes" would be needed and the crunch finally came in the middle of the eighteenth century. In 1767 Rector Stanley, possibly having in mind the need of accommodation whilst rebuilding the Parish Church, appointed eight trustees to oversee the building of St. John's as the Chapel-of-Ease. On the 8th June, 1770, the new Chapel was consecrated by the Bishop of Chester. Outwardly it was plain with a meagre bell turret at the West End but the interior revealed a fine proportioned Church with a gallery round three sides supported by floor-to-ceiling columns and a shallow apse with a Venetian window at the East End.

The Chapel was officially built by public subscription and under the deeds of consecration such contributors were rewarded with an assigned "sitting" in perpetuity for the annual fee of one shilling. The Rector maintained the right to appoint the Minister-in-charge at St. John's and he has continued to hold the Patronage since the Parish was formed in 1862. One Minister, the Rev. Campbell, had one of his Baptism Services interrupted by an unsuspected event — an earthquake. In 1777 we are told "a terrible shock of earthquake was felt". Even though Mr. Campbell endeavoured to assure the congregation there was nothing to fear a stampede broke out as people rushed into the Chapel yard leaving a scene of devastation. Another recorded event in the annals of the Chapelry was when the Bishop of Chester visited it in 1821. The Lord Bishop of the Diocese was disturbed at what he saw and ordered the Minister to have the Bible rebound and the Church whitewashed. Not content with a simple decor required by Episcopal order the Church was whitewashed, the columns painted in colour, green blinds fitted to the windows and a Venetian blind to the East window. In those sparse days the beautified St. John's must have been a colourful spectacle.

In 1956 the final chapter of Bury's finest Church building came to be written. It was found that during the one hundred and eighty years' life of the old Chapel the industrial grime had eaten into the stonework which had been laid wrongly in the first instance. Firms refused to commit themselves to a contract price for its restoration and the decision was taken to build a new Church beside the existing Mission near to the centre of the Parish for when the boundaries of the Parishes were first delineated the line went round St. John's in the Rock at the southern most tip of the assigned area. No Christian congregation is a keeper of historic buildings and wisdom prevailed. The Vicar, the Rev. Arthur Hulse, accepted the responsibility of beginning a new St. John's whilst watching the demolition of the old Chapel. The demolishers had early assistance from wanton vandalism. It is sad that the oldest public building in Bury and certainly its finest piece of architecture passed on to the silent pages of history but the Church, as a limb of the Body of Christ, continues and perhaps another author will pen the records of the new building and its worshippers in another two-hundred years.

This booklet was produced by the

Bury Times

brochure department

We will be pleased to receive

enquiries for similar publications

Bury Times Brochure Dept.
Cross Street
Bury
Telephone 061-764 5063

Branch Offices at Radcliffe and Whitefield

CHAPTER 4—INTO THE HILL COUNTRY

To travel from Manchester to Whalley on foot or horseback would take at least two days, and that ignoring the hazards and dangers which pilgrims to the ancient Abbey could face. In order to provide a place of refuge for the night, Abbeys built small Chantry Chapels which could be termed "a pilgrim's praying station". There are few left in England and none still standing in Lancashire.

Holcombe

The Priory of Monk Bretton, a Cluniac Monastery near Barnsley in Yorkshire was bequeathed the whole of "Holcombe forest" by Roger Montbegon in A.D. 1225. In this transaction there is a reference to ". . . . a solid simple block of sand-stone" as a landmark within the vast estates of de Lacy ,Earl of Lincoln. The "Pilgrim's Cross" as it became called was stolen in 1901 and all that remains to-day is the foundation stone with the square well which once housed the base of the cross. It could have been erected by travelling monks to guide their way between the Monasteries and the Churches where they ministered.

Holcombe was renouned for the shelter it offered to travellers. The name itself is significant as "Hol" is the Saxon word for "a hollow" or "deep" and "Cwm" a valley or bosom of a hill, a word still extensively used in Wales. In this deep hollow, below the Pilgrim's Cross, the Prior and Convocation of Monk Bretton built a Chantry Chapel. Some-times licenses were granted to such chantries for the saying of Mass and the preaching of Sermons, and especially if they were to serve as a Chapel-of-Ease for the area. This could well have been the case at Holcombe as a Curate once told a Bishop's Commission that the joint duties of Holcombe and Edenfield for which he was responsible " . . . . were computed to be one third of the whole Parish of Bury". Chantry priests had a rigorous existence. A coarse frieze cassock to keep them warm and a dagger for self-defence as they journeyed between the isolated hamlets.

The sixteenth century was a stormy time for Church and State. In 1537 Whalley Abbey was "captured" by the Earl of Derby and the Abbot duly executed at Lancaster. No longer was the Church all-powerful but subjected to the Laws of the Realm as an individual person. In 1546, the first year of the reign of King Edward VI, chan-tries were suppressed as they were open to considerable abuse and superstition and the priests retired on a pittance of a pension, so ended Holcombe Chantry as such. The building and its ornaments were left intact for it is recorded in the Inventory of Church goods, 1552, that Holcombe had "Two vestements, one of satayn of brygges (evidently Bruges in Flanders were satin was made) with a red crosse of saye. An oy' of blocke saye with a redde crosse of chamlett . . . . a bell in the chappell and a sacryng bell. An old surples and a pax of brasse". All these were sold on 1st April, 1553, for £3 6s. 8d. Holcombe had no Minister and no Chapel but the Rev. Richard Jones, Rector of Bury, spoke in his will of 1568 about "gatheryne of my tythe corne money in the fforest".

A new Chapel was consecrated in the reign of Queen Elizabeth I although the building was originally a prison and complaints were lodged in 1717 that the Lords of the Manor continued to exercise their feudal privilege of executing prisoners within its precincts, perhaps not the best meditation before worship! A court for the Royal Manor of Tottington was held at Harwood Fields and within the lands adjoining this house is Castle Hill House. The rear portion of this building shows

The Judges' Window : Castle Hill House

considerable evidence that it was once used as the Court Room and prison. Nearby is Gallows' Hill reputed to be the scene of many gruesome spectacles as the Law was seen to be done.

Holcombe and Edenfield were treated as one in the Middle Ages. The Bishop of Chester took a "Notitia Cestriensis" circa 1714-1725 and states "Eatonfield or Eadenfield. Certif. £00 05. 00 par given by John Grime. 5 m. Bury. 2 m. Holcombe. Same curate supplies both . . . . both of them were consecrated in Queen Elizabeth's reign. In reign of Charles I the Bishop compelled each Chapelry to allow £10 p.a. a piece ye minister when sh'd chose or sh'd send to officiate once a month in each chap. but now there are only contrib. of about £8 p.a. to both".

The "prison-chapel" at Holcombe (for want of a better description) was enlarged in 1714 when the old oak benches were converted into a reading desk and Churchwardens' pew. It was enlarged again in 1774 and finally demolished in 1851. The existing Church was consecrated on 8th April, 1853, by the first Bishop of Manchester, the Rt. Rev. Prince Lee.

38

Life in the hill country was hard. A tragic story comes from the 14th century when one of Henry de Lacy's soldiers who had fought against the Scots at Falkirk (1298) killed a fawn in the forest to alleviate the hunger of his family. A herdsman watched the poacher and denounced him to the Lord of the Manor. He was duly hanged at Holcombe and his body allowed to dangle from the gibbet for some days. In a pleasanter vein comes the story of the poor farm lad who made good. In 1760 the Rev. James Wood, D.D., became Dean of Ely and Master of St. John's College, Cambridge. In his early days James walked three miles every morning "in clogs" to Bury Grammar School. He bequeathed £500 to his old school for the augmentation of the Kay Exhibitions, he himself having received help as an exhibitioner.

Hey House built in 1616 : The De Trafford's Hunting Lodge

Photo : "Bury Times".

Hey House — One of the oldest houses at Holcombe was built in 1616 and then taken over in 1617 by the influential de Trafford family as a hunting lodge in the forest of Holcombe. One of the crests in the small stained glass windows is the Leopard's Head of the De Traffords and inside the lounge are examples of wood panelling and pews reputed to have been imported from Whalley Abbey in 1635. Side wings have been added but Hey House is very little different from the day when King James I paid a visit. The house has a long association with the Holcombe Hunt and a painting over the fireplace, by Fearnley, is of James Kenyon, huntsman in 1780.

The Leopard's Head of the De Traffords.

Edenfield

The ancient Parish of Bury stretched from Radcliffe in the south to Rossendale in the north. The village of Cowpe, near Waterfoot, was within its boundaries primarily because it is the point where the trail across the moors from Bury to Newchurch descended into the Valley, once part of the Royal Forest of Rossendale.

A village which grew up at the junction of another trade route is Edenfield, which supported one of Bury's four Chapels-of-Ease. The County Archivist has stated that a Chapel was in Edenfield in the 13th century and therefore must have its beginnings almost as soon as the other Chapel-in-the-Hills, Holcombe. The Chapel is again on record in 1553 when two people were involved in a court case for " . . . . assault in Edenfield Chapel". During the following century the Commonwealth Survey, held under the directive of Oliver Cromwell recommended that Edenfield should become a Parish in its own right but, like so many of these schemes, it was shelved at the Restoration. A Parish was finally formed in the nineteenth century during the division of the ancient Parish.

If Edenfield suffered from the Restoration she could hardly plead special favour for loyalty. In the Church is a bell dated 1654 which was cast by John Scott of Wigan. Although bells were prohibited by the Commonwealth Parliament, Edenfield was able to obtain one and it did noble service until replaced in 1920 by eight bells, rung as a carillon. The tower of the Church was extended in 1614 and could be termed "the leaning tower of ancient Bury" for in its height of 43 feet there is a deviation from the vertical of 23 inches. The Chapel was

Hey House : a corner seat reputed to be a converted pew from Whalley Abbey.

Edenfield Church exterior

Edenfield Church : Interior

42

rebuilt in 1778 (the date is on a stone set into the East Wall) but not without considerable clerical pressure. A meeting was called by the Curate-in-Charge to discuss the urgency of the situation. All agreed that rebuilding was necessary but no agreement could be reached on how the project was to be financed. The meeting adjourned and summoned once more, this time under the threat that if no scheme was agreed there would be no more Services until such time as a plan or offers were forthcoming. The end of the second meeting was the same as the first and the Curate carried out his threat and closed the Chapel until some satisfactory conclusion had been reached. The notice which he pinned to the Church door is still in existence.

There is in the keeping of the Vicar the notebook of the Rev. John Smith who was Minister of both Holcombe and Edenfield for nearly fifty years, from 1764 to 1810. It is entitled "This book contains extracts of various ecclesiastical laws and other useful memorandums for the Manor of Tottington". This is "Light on the Times". The Churchwardens had to examine every corpse before burial to ensure it was covered by a woollen shroud — an early example of trade protection ! There is also the estimates "For digging a navigation from Sowerby Bridge to Manchester" by James Brindley, the famous illiterate engineer of the Bridgewater Canal. Brindley suggested two alternative routes : the first followed the line upon which it was eventually built and the other came through Bamford, Hooley Bridge to the River Roach and then along the basin of the Irwell to Manchester. This great undertaking was estimated to cost £138,000.

One or two quotations, besides the above references, will show the range of this man's interest.

Articles 1763, June 3, paid to Mr. Pilkington, of Manchester, for one wigg. 16s. 0d.

Recipes. For the cure of dropsy.
An excellent prescription.

Let 2 ounces of Jesuit's bark, 2 ounces of Battal gunpowder, and 2 ounces of Corn Mustard Seed, be steeped in a quart of Sweet Mountain Wine, and shaken well together. And let 3 wine glasses be taken every day.

Texts and Comments on burials.

1792 Holcombe April 24. James Lomax, Bolton.
Psalm 71, 20. Killed by a cart. Aged 73.

1793 Giles Hoyle lost in a storm, February 13th Holcombe Stubbins Higher Hill. Psalm 103, 15.

Edenfield was a thriving community being in the midst of a sheep rearing area and it had its own school as early as 1728, later rebuilt in 1860. One of the claims in the petition seeking a grant towards the cost of rebuilding was the antiquity of its foundation.

The Mediaeval village time-piece.   The Sundial on the South Wall, Edenfield Church.

44

Ancient Halls

Edenfield village, surrounding the Church, stands high above the River Irwell commanding a fine view of the hill country, whilst down the valley, and within a short distance, as the crow flies, is Lumb Hall, the oldest unspoilt building still standing in the ancient Parish of Bury and may well have been of sufficient importance to cause Edenfield Chapel to be first established as a private chantry chapel. The Mediaeval stone exterior of the Hall, recently stripped of its plaster rendering, gives no hint of the wooden crucks which form the central support for the two storey house. In a document which passed between the Earl of Derby and the Rawsthornes in the 15th century there is reference to a timber structure standing on the land at Lumb. It would appear that the outer walls were rebuilt in stone around the "heart" of this building which was then about two-hundred years old and this is the Hall which still stands today on the banks of the Irwell. For nearly 400 years the Hall was associated with the Rawsthorne family beginning with John who first claimed land in 1292 from Richard de Shuttleworth. In those far off days land was always in dispute and John's grandson, another John, had to defend a claim against the land by Agnes de Shuttleworth. It is known that in 1482 Adam Rawsthorne lived in Lumb Hall, the earliest reference to the actual house. The eldest sons continued to inherit Lumb for nearly two hundred years when the estate was conveyed in the marrage of Elizabeth to a Thomas Bradshaw in 1660. Elizabeth's grandfather had left seven silver spoons to remain as family heirlooms in the ancestral home but the long dynasty of Lumb Hall was to end. Edenfield, however, still had a Rawsthorne family in residence for in 1538 a branch of the family, which originated in Tottington, purchased New Hall. It was Lawrence Rawsthorne of Old Windsor who bought this historic homestead, which was, like Lumb, typical of the small free-holders' or yeoman farmers' houses of the Mediaeval days. Lawrence's son, Edward, was involved with the Royalists during the Civil War and assisted in the defence of Lathom House in 1644-45. To-day no Rawsthornes are found in either Hall. Lumb has been well restored as a private residence, whilst the Irwell Valley Water Board (now amalgamated with the Bolton Water Undertaking) saved New Hall from complete destruction and have restored part of the building as a filter house. The roots of our life are dug deep and it is gratifying to realise that some remains of our past have been preserved in the hill country.

Walmersley

Today's route north from Bury is very different from former years. At a place called Pigs Lee the old coach road made its way through the village of Baldingstone onto the remote and bleak Harden Moor, whilst the modern macadam ribbon hugs the side of the Irwell Valley. The old road has a haunting fascination for those who care to use it. It passes the occasional ancient house and garden isolated in the silence of moorland space as an oasis in a desert. Time has ravaged the route, now partly destroyed by encroaching quarries near Shuttleworth, and lacking in its commuters to the one-time thriving cotton industry of Deeply Vale and Bircle Dene.

Lumb Hall: the seat of the Rawsthorne family

Photo: "Bury Times".

Buckhurst Chapel-School

In 1838 to provide a spiritual Ministry to the Valley industry, the first new Parish was formed in the ancient Parish of Bury, the Parish of Walmersley. The needs were such that two new buildings were necessary besides continuing to use the Baldingstone "Penny School". This old school was founded in 1715 and financed by the fee paying pupils, at the weekly rate of one penny. It was staffed by a Headmaster who received the salary of £15 per annum and for much of the time he was aided by a lady assistant.

A Church was built beside the new road, near to its junction with the coach route and this served the parishioners for fifty years when it was replaced by the present neo-Gothic building designed by Maxwell and Tuke in 1883. The first Church was sparse and devoid of the many ecclesiastical embellishments which came in vogue in the later half of the nineteenth century. Inside, the maximum seating accommodation was afforded by a gallery, not an unusual feature of the time. The East Window of the first Church was preserved and built into the new building, now standing on the site of its predecessor.

The Church at the centre of the Parish necessitated a school much nearer to the industrial population. In the same year as the Parish was formed the moorland Buckhurst School was opened. Again an unpretentious functional building to provide education for the children in the week and licensed for Services on the Sabbath. It was originally a one-class school, all ages together and taught by the one teacher. After World War II it became a Junior School and won fame for its pupils going to school on their ponies. In 1880 Buckhurst seemed to have outlived its usefulness as the cotton workers evacuated the valley but earned a reprieve when the reservoir near "O'wd Betts" was constructed. This new life continued away beyond the completion of that project in 1904 but its doors finally closed in 1965 when the last service was held on Easter Sunday.

A stage-coach in 1837 from a painting by J. Shaver

By courtesy of H.M. Post Master General.

By Stage :-

Before the Industrial Revolution Bury was virtually an outpost north of Manchester. It was a convenient distance from the city to provide a stopping place for travellers to Clitheroe, Skipton and beyond. Because of the strategic distance the Market Place became a cluster of coaching inns, hostelries and alehouses. A book published in 1824 entitled "History of the Borough of Bury" has preserved the time-table for the stage coaches and their respective inns. Each run had its own name such as "The Waterloo Comet" and "The Resolution" — a practice which was later copied by the railway companies. The two foremost inns were "The Greymare" facing the Market Place and demolished in 1836 and the "Eagle and Child" in Silver Street. Destinations as far afield as Liverpool and Hull were served from Bury and the thought of such a journey must have made even the hardiest travellers wince as they boarded the coaches. A regular service ran between Bury and Manchester on Tuesdays and Thursdays but the Rochdale-Bury-Manchester service was discontinued in 1796 due to lack of patronage.

Old Grey Mare

By Water :-

As the stage-coach rumbled out of the Market Place towards Liverpool its route lay along the narrow "Bury Lane" down to Bury Bridge. Beside the bridge stood the "Ship Inn" which was periodically transformed into a court-room for visiting magistrates from Bolton. This court dealt with many of the petty offences in the town and was later moved to the "Red Lion", which stood next to the Parish Church. In 1824 William Grant was appointed as Bury's first resident Justice of the Peace which brought an end to these temporary courts although Lancaster remained the scene of the Assize Courts.

The Warf Warehouse : Bury Bridge.

The tow path near Elton Paper Works.

Another feature near to Bury Bridge was the head of the Manchester, Bolton and Bury Canal which was first used to carry coal into the town on 24th September, 1796. It is today in a state of disuse and and the old warehouse over one of the three wharfs stands derelict. By today's standards the horse drawn barge was slow but in the eighteenth century it was no slower than land transport and it was far easier to carry large volumes of bulk cargo. The narrow hump-back bridges, often locally nicknamed "the camel's hump" were designed to allow the horse to plod its way along the towpath without hindrance. Industrialists took advantage of canals and some built their mills along the banks, often building their own private wharf. Cruising down the canal on a Sunday afternoon was a relief for many of the cotton and woollen workers of Bury. Unfortunately this form of relaxation came to an abrupt end when some drunken revellers sank a pleasure boat near the quay, drowning a number of passengers.

Canals were originally given their more proper name of "Navigations". They were dug out by hand and many Irish immigrants came over to do this work. These labourers became affectionately known as "Navvies" and as they settled on English soil brought with them their religious faith and traditions. Many Roman Catholic Churches have their beginnings in the era of canal and railway construction and St. Marie's in Bury was no exception. Built in 1841 it has been the centre of a large Roman Catholic community in the town. Interestingly enough co-operation between Churches is nothing new. The architect, John Harper of York, designed both St. Marie's and the Parish Church of All Saints : Elton. The Roman Catholic Church stands prominently

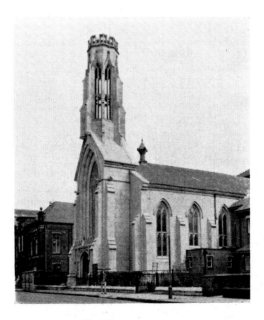

St. Marie's lantern

on Silver Street with its lantern tower, based on the central feature of Ely Cathedral, over the West door. Besides their religion the Irish brought some of their traditions. Bury with its prolific number of brew-houses provided a ready breeding ground for the "Irish Wakes" which finally died out in the 1870's. The tradition was to mourn the death of a relative by an all-night drinking party, the guests including the corpse set up in its coffin. The joint efforts of Bury clergy were so effective that it is doubtful if many people know of the "Wakes" today, except those who still have family ties in Ireland where it is still celebrated.

By Rail :-

In our imagination we can see the excitement caused 123 years ago as the local farmers or factory workers saw their first steam-train travel from Bolton through to Heywood, which left Bury at 8-0 a.m. "'As ta sen th' iron awse, Bill o' Ben?" asked Jock o' Ted on the night 1st May, 1848 in the local brew-house. "Nah" replied Bill "but I't heart whistle as I were a milkin'." Jock had been down early near to Heap Bridge. He went on "I did no' leek luk o' wuden bridge o'er ditch — it seem't sheeft a bit". Bill added his little knowledge "Them do sy it cud go abeet fowty miles in t'owr".

Heywood was first linked to the growing rail network in 1841 by a branch line, served with horse-drawn trains, from the Manchester-Leeds Railway which had overcome the Pennines in 1838 by what George Stephenson called "the greatest piece of railway engineering which had been accomplished to date". (Before the Blue Pits (now Castleton) to Heywood line was built the passengers travelled the distance by canal). Eventually the Manchester-Leeds Railway was to become the largest partner in the Lancashire-Yorkshire Railway Comapny when it was formed by a group of Companies in 1859. However, it was not the first in the field, that honour goes to the Manchester, Bolton and Bury Railway. The proprietors of the canal which linked the three towns received Parliamentary sanction in 1831 to drain their canal and construct the rail-road in its bed. The practical outworking of the idea for building the railway was not quite as easy as first appearance seemed and so many deviations became necessary that the route was completely abandoned and a new one planned. The Manchester-Bolton section opened in 1838 but for some inexplicable reason the six miles from Bolton to Bury were not built and it was 1845 before a railway ran through Bury but then by a completely different company.

The Manchester, Bury and Rossendale Railway was one of the three parent companies of the East Lancashire Railway who had their head offices and railway works at Bury and they remained independent from the L. & Y. Railway for some thirteen years. The vision to link Heywood and Bury belonged to the East Lancashire who instructed their consulting engineer, Mr. Hawkshaw, to survey the branch line between the two towns. Plans advanced and in February 1845 the Company ordered its Solicitors to introduce a Bill into Parliament for building the line and they reported back that this had been done. The reason why this scheme failed may have been due to the "double

Lancashire and Yorkshire Railway : Bridge at Bury over the Heywood Branch Extension Railway.

Print reproduced by kind permission of Borough Librarian.

The offices of the East Lancashire Railway Co. at Bolton Street Station

dealings" by Mr. Hawkshaw. The engineer resigned his post with the East Lancashire in December 1844 after so being invited " . . . in view of his present obligation to support the Leeds Co. in their application for a Branch Railway from Bury to Heywood".

The typical Victorian stone buildings of what is now Bolton Street Station have the convincing air of grandeur and reliability. It is not difficult to picture the heavily-moustached station master meeting the carriage of some local dignitary at the entrance facade. Some of the local "magnets" would take their whole household on holiday by rail and accommodation was obviously provided to meet this traffic.

In the 1840's the clamour of the rail rush caused Parliament to pass Acts for the building of railways at a phenomenal pace. These sometimes brought vicious competition between Companies and equal jealousy amongst their financiers. One battle blew up when a group of industralists in 1844 seeking Parliamentary sanction, proposed to join the mid-Lancashire towns of Wigan and Bolton to Liverpool and, as an after-thought added Bury. The new railway to be known as the Liverpool-Bury Railway. The East Lancashire Railway saw the inevitable build-up of the cross-country route if it linked with Heywood and forbade the new railway any right of way across their own track and so the underpass, which still stands, came to be built.

The famous railway engineer Robert Stephenson had said that in his opinion 40 m.p.h. was as fast as a train should ever want to go and it is certain the early thin-boilered Locomotive would not reach that speed as it pulled its load up the 130 feet difference between Bury and Heywood. The three viaducts on the run from Bolton are of some interest. The timber bridge over the River Roach, near Heap Bridge, lasted only 14 years when it was replaced by the brick "Seven Arches" at a cost of £3,491. A more exhilarating experience is crossing the two viaducts nearer to Bolton, the Burnden and the Darcy-Lever.

The Darcy Lever Viaduct

Both these are built of lattice girders and the Darcy-Lever, which crosses the River Tonge at a height of 86 feet consists of six spans of 84 feet and two of 54 feet — some achievement.

Competition for custom was fierce. In the report of the opening of the line and the new Heywood Station in the *Manchester Guardian* (3rd May, 1848) it says "It is intended to run from Manchester to Bury 'in ½ hour" which is the time occupied in going between the two places by the East Lancs. line . . . . . Bury is now, by this branch, connected with all the great markets of the West Riding and with Rochdale". When the line opened there was only "a temporary erection as a station at Bury" but it wasn't long before the once fine-looking platforms of Bury Knowsley Street were built. The line finally closed on Saturday, 3rd October, 1970.

Any traveller through Heywood cannot fail to notice the shard curve of the line which is also reflected in the station canopy and platform. It was a proud boast of Mr. Thompson, the Contractor, that the branch line at Heywood met "head on" with the Bury link. However it is suggested the original station was about "one quarter of a mile" from the present structure and the sharp curve was necessary to fulfil Mr. Thompson's dream of a direct meeting.

Heywood Station—now demolished

The free competition between companies had both its blessings and misgivings. On the one hand safety was often neglected for speed whilst every comfort was lavished upon the passenger. In 1845 the East Lancashire resolved to follow the example of the Birmingham group and upholster their 1st class carriages with drab cloth.

Industry was developing fast and the growth of the paper works on the banks of the Roach was speeded by the advent of the railway. In 1860 the Lancashire & Yorkshire Railway Co. asked for estimates to build a branch line to Heap Bridge. The cost was to be about £8,000, plans were produced and notice given that the line was to be built. For twelve years nothing happened and when the contract was awarded to Dransfield and Holme of Liverpool the sum had risen to £11,500. Eventually the cost was well over £20,000 since the original mile length was extended to Mr. Wrigley's works (now Transparent Papers) and this total included a large retaining wall costing over £5,000 which

No. 746 "Thor". One of a class of four 2-4-0 locomotives built at the E.L.Rly.
works in Bury, 1875. The couples wheels were 5ft. 6in. in diameter.

Photo by courtesy of Borough Librarian.

"Seven Arches" railway viaduct across the River Roach

"Mr. Wrigley will have to reimburse, as he has founded his warehouse on it". This expensive branch serves both Transparent Papers and Yates Duxbury and the latter firm still runs two steam engines — typical of the industrial motive power at the turn of the century.

Passing Bury Gas Works Sidings box, a standard class "2" 2-6-0 No. 78043 on its way to Wigan.

Photo by I. G. Holt.

Knowsley Street Station. A Stanier 4-6-0 No. 45101 rides over the hump, 1962.

Photo by R. S. Greenwood.

By Tram :-

As the canal brought goods in bulk, the railways brought prosperity and work. The town continued to expand, one area grew into the next until there was little demarcation between the communities. It soon became evident that some form of inner transport was needed and some Bury business men joined with other local townsfolk to form the Manchester, Bury, Rochdale and Oldham Steam Tramways in 1882. The first steam tram ran on 12th March, 1883, from Bury Market Place to Blackford Bridge. This early line used the same track gauge as the railway of 4ft. 8½in. The next two ventures of lines to Tottington and Heap Bridge used the narrower gauge of 3ft. 6in. The whole enterprise was so successful that in 1897 they were running a fleet of 107 locos. and 96 cars. Problems awaited the "steamers". The concentration of fumes in the desperately narrow streets led to violent objections, so much so that when a track was laid to Limefield popular demand ensured it was horse-drawn until 1886.

A steam tram of the Bury, Rochdale and Oldham Steam Tramways
Photo by courtesy of Tramway Museum, Crich.

In March, 1896 the Steam Tram Company applied to the Corporation for permission to replace the steam system by electric traction but the Council had considerable misgivings about allowing a private company to organise the town's transport and so it resoved to buy-out the Steam Company and run its own trams. On 3rd June, 1903, Bury Corporation Tramways opened the first section of its electric system from Moorside to Jericho : six employees being the total labour force of Bury Corporation's first week as a transport authority. At that moment in time both the Steam and Electric trams were running in the town although the relationship between the two bodies was very tense and had deteriorated over the Company's indifference to maintaining the road surface. The Steam Tram Co. was, on 24th February, 1904, fragmented when the various local authorities took over their particular interests in the private concern,purchased at a cost inflated by the arbitrator. Within a week new work was in progress. The first need was to electrify the existing lines. The Heap Bridge run opened on 21st April, 1904, and Limefield on 29th of the same month, these were followed by the Tottington service on 16th September, 1904. The trams were handsomely painted in red and cream and over the years Bury had a fleet of 60 such cars.

In 1925 a new form of transport invaded Bury — buses. On 18th September a single deck Leyland bus linked Walshaw and destiny has shown that the motorised transport was to replace the tram. In March, 1933, the Council approved a plan to gradually replace the trams as the maintenance of the permanent way was proving increasingly expensive. The last tram ran to Walmersley on 13th February, 1949. The last coach, the last canal barge, the last steam train and the last tram have all ploughed their way to Bury providing its necessary life-link with the world outside. Each invention played its part until its use was outworn and could be replaced with more efficient means. The fruits of those earlier efforts have provided the things of today and perhaps the present advancements will ultimately replace what we so richly enjoy.

Interior of Depot, taken in 1903, showing types of cars then used

Tottington High Street in 1937

Photo by H. B. Priestly by permission of the Tramway Museum Society.

By Trackless Electric Tram Car:-

The final experiment for some means of public transport, before the universal introduction of the motor bus, was a vehicle entitled "the Trackless Electric Tram Car" which was introduced by the Ramsbottom Urban District Council to serve its own locality. There had been an Act of Parliament entitled the "Tramways Order Confirmation (No. 2)" passed in 1903 to authorise the building of an electric tramway but due to the estimated high financial outlay for a relatively small passenger potential the whole scheme was abandoned.

After further deliberation the decision was taken to provide a "Trackless Tram" transport system and the 1912 Railless Traction Act gave the Council the necessary permission. Work began and on Thursday, 14th August, 1913, at 6-0 p.m. the first car ran to Holcombe Brook. Ramsbottom can lay claim to be one of the first municipalities to run its entire transport system by trolley bus (the name which was later used for the trackless tram). This situation continued for the next ten years when a new service was envisaged to link Edenfield with both Rawtenstall and the Walmersley Tram terminus in Bury. Three motor buses were purchased in August, 1923. During the 1920's the Ramsbottom undertaking had a difficult passage due to pressure from the privately owned Ribble Motor Services Ltd., inter-working with other authorities and the continual financial loss of the trolley buses. The low maintenance of the motor bus compared with the trolley bus for a small service was to sound the death-knell of the trackless tram. Equipment was not renewed and on 31st March, 1931, the project was finally abandoned.

No. 1.   Trackless Electric Tram at Holcombe Brook.

Although the Ramsbottom Traction Committee only ran one major route, from Holcombe Brook to Edenfield with a short branch between the railway station and the Market Place they were pioneers in a mode of transport which became popular in many cities, including Manchester. It is perhaps some consolation to the initial optimism which brought the trolley bus to Ramsbottom to realise that Manchester did not introduce its first trolley bus until 1938 and perhaps as a testimony we could change the Mancunians' well worn adage "What Ramsbottom did today, Manchester does tomorrow!"

CHAPTER 5—ACROSS THE RIVER

Bury Bridge across the River Irwell

Fording the River Irwell from Bury one immediately enters the area of Elton. The road to Bolton continues straight on but the journey to Walshaw, Tottington or Edenfield was thwarted with problems at the junction of the three roads. To get the travellers on the right road a sign post was erected in 1834. Surrounding this road junction there had grown up a small hamlet which erupted in the late 1850's and '60's into a densely populated area with the opening up of the paper industry at Elton Paper Mills and Walmsleys Engineering but the name and fame of Elton extends from days much earlier than either of these enterprises.

The name Elton never belonged to a feudal lord or baron ruling his estate from some ancient hall but it was used in the 13th Century by a local family. Like many other land-owners the Eltons had a dispute with Adam de Bury. In 1278 Alexander de Elton and his son were defendants to a claim by Adam over their land, but it was shown that Adam had never had legal possession of the tenement in dispute and so the Eltons continued to enjoy their rights.

Within the land originally owned by the Elton family there was built the manor house of Brandlesholme and adjacent farm, which had forty-eight acres of land attached. Brandlesholme was a family name whose surviving member, Alice, conveyed the estate, in marriage, to Henry Greenhalgh during the reign of King Richard II (1377-1399). The expanse of the Manor covered the border country between Tottington and Bury for both Alice and Henry made settlements of the estate in both places in 1397 and 1398. The Greenhalgh's reigned at Brandlesholme for about four hundred years, the most famous member being

This Portrait of JOHN GREENHALGH of Brandlesome,
(who governed and maintained tranquility in the Isle of Man, from 16.. to 1651,)
was saved, during the Earthquake that occurred on the Island of Juan Fernandes, and is dedicated to

The Right Hon.ble Earl of Derby

by his obedient humble Servant.

Ent. Sta. Hall

The Brave and unfortunate James Earl of Derby's Character of Governor Greenhalgh, and his reasons for his Choice of him:
First, That he was a Gentleman well born, and such usually scorn a base action. Secondly, That he has a good Estate of his own, and therefore need not borrow of another which hath been a Fault in this Country; for when Governors have wanted, and been forced to be beholding to those who may be the greatest gainers against the Lord and Country; in such Case the Borrower becomes Servant to the Lender; to the Stoppage, if not the Perversion of Justice; next he was a Deputy Lieutenant and Justice of Peace for his own County; he govern'd his own Affairs well, & therefore was the more likely to do mine as he hath been approved Prudent and Valiant; and as such fitter to be trusted, in fine he is such that I think is't for him, and charge you to Love him as a Friend.

Barrow's History of the House of Stanley, and Baines's History of the County Palatine of Lancaster.

John, who was Governor of the Isle of Man from 1640-1651. His appointment was made in the reign of Charles I and he continued into the Commonwealth period until he died in 1651 in exile. It is known that one of John's ancestors, Thomas, who died in 1576, held the Manor from the Earl of Derby and this was one of the estates in Lancashire which the Parliamentarians seized from the Royalist sympathisers.

Brandlesholme Hall by "Clock" Shaw. Mr. Shaw painted many views of Bury at the end of the last century and was nicknamed "Clock" due to the clock on his shop in the Market Place.

The reasons why John Greenhalgh was appointed to this high office are interesting. A citation reads "he was a Gentleman well born, and such usually scorn a base action : secondly, That he has a good Estate of his own, and therefore need not borrow from another . . . . next he was Deputy Lieutenant and Justice of the Peace for his own county : he governed his own Affairs well . . . . he hath been approved Prudent and Valient, and as such fitter to be trusted in fine". He must have been approved by King and Parliament alike for his statesmanship and even with the uprising and down-fallings of Monarchs and governments the Greenhalghs maintained possession of Brandlesholme until about 1770 when it was sold to a Richard Powell, merchant of Heaton Norris.

The old hall was as "a good specimen of the half-timbered gabled houses of the district" probably built in the 15th or 16th Century. It was a large dwelling for in 1666 when a tax was taken, Thomas Greenhalgh had 12 hearths out of a total of 75 in Elton. (Another contributor in this tax was Roger Kay of Woodhill, no doubt father of the Grammar School's benefactor). The fireplace which stood in the banqueting hall of Brandlesholme is still to be seen with the rope rack for the spit and the circular turning mark showing where the serf stood to cook the boar. A small recess in one corner is thought to be the Minstrels' gallery which may have once extended over the hearth but its present size is adequate to hold the small group of travelling musicians which would periodically visit the Hall on its tours. The front of the hall was destroyed by fire near the turn of this century and rebuilt in Victorian fashion but certain remaining interior features reflect the way of life once enjoyed by the Greenhalghs

Brandlesholme Hall is still isolated at the norther tip of Elton whilst the industrial and housing development has taken place near to Bury Bridge. Whilst the township was still in its infancy the Parish

The Minstrels' Gallery: Brandlesholme Hall

All Saints', Elton, 1864.

Church of All Saints' was opened in 1843 on a field called "Goose Hill Bank". It took nearly two years to build at a cost of £2,500 which was met by public subscription. A licence was granted by the Diocese of Chester on 14th March, 1843, to use the building for Divine Services and it was first used on 30th April. On 1st June the Earl of Derby conveyed the land, and the buildings which stood on it, by a Deed Poll to the Rector of Bury. Finally it was consecrated on 29th June (St. Peter's Day) by the Bishop of Chester, and Elton was assigned as a separate ecclesiastical district on 13th December by an Order in Council.

All Saints' is one Church about which no one can say "It's not like it used to be" because it is nearly impossible to depict what the Church was like at its Consecration. The west porch has been added : the original entrances in the north and south transepts blocked up : the organ which stood in the west gallery was transported to Bircle in 1884 and a new organ and chamber built : pews have been replaced at regular intervals, the two most important occasions were, firstly, in 1895 when the choir pews were installed as a memorial to the Rev. E. Westerman, Vicar for 32 years, and, secondly, in 1965, when the pews from St. John's in the Rock reseated the Nave.

Following the Church, Elton was soon to have its own school. In 1845 land was assigned by Lord Derby to be "appropriated and used as and for a school or schools for education of Children and Adults or children only of labouring, manufacturing and other poorer classes in the township of Elton. . . . . and as a residence for the school-master and school-mistress and for no other purpose". When the school closed and the Church took over the premises for a Parish Hall, the land had to be purchsed from Lord Derby to comply with these conditions. A Boys' and Girls' School opened on 4th September, 1847, under the headships of Mr. and Miss Haigh. The Headmaster was replaced after only one year by a Mr. Hull but Miss Haigh continued to the winter of 1850. There are complete records of both Church and School preserved at the Church.

As the Parish expanded along Bolton Road the daughter Church of St. Stephen's was built to form the focal point of a separate Parish. When the new Church was consecrated in 1884 there was no Communion plate so a paton and chalice were lent by All Saints' for the Service. Possession is nine-tenths of the law and there is considerable correspondence between the Bishop and Vicar proposing to have a replica chalice made and exchanging it for the original. A replica was certainly made but the hall-marks indicate that the original never returned "home".

Walshaw

Beyond the immediate perimeter of any township small villages sprang up. One such place was Walshaw, at one time centred in its hall but in the 1840's monopolised by the two cotton concerns of the Haworth's and the Holt's. Of the Holts I have no information but when the Haworths came to Walshaw they began a general store, which also included rooms for hand weavers. As trade increased they moved across the road and manufactured fustian from the raw cotton. The cotton famine of 1860 brought many problems into the village, as elsewhere. The business was controlled by Jesse Haworth who, by careful planning, continued to provide a day's work each week which,

Walshaw showing Jesse Haworth's Memorial Church
Photo: "Bury Times"

at least, helped to maintain the skill of his operatives. For the day's work he alleviated the acute poverty by paying two day's wages and, on request, he willingly lent another day's. To save the community from the greatest problem — boredom, he provided classes in the school in reading and writing for men and "domestic subjects" for the women during the idle days.

The nephew of Jesse Haworth, John Gorell Haworth, was instrumental in writing the family name indelibly on the village. In April, 1847, he established a Sunday School in Walshaw for teaching the doctrines of the Church of England, as opposed to the Methodist connection which began cira 1838, and later that same year he entered St. Aidan's Theological College, Birkenhead, to study for the Ministry. In 1851 the now Rev. J. G. Haworth was instituted as Vicar of Holy Trinity, Tunstead, in the Rossendale Valley, but his interest continued in Walshaw. When his Uncle Jesse died in 1887 he planned with an Aunt, Nancy Haworth, to build an Anglican Church in Walshaw of which he would be Patron with "his heirs and assigns". The "Jesse Haworth Memorial Church" was consecrated in 1889, the same year in which "J. G." resigned his Tunstead living, and the Order in Council forming the Parish announced that for the ". . . . . purpose of providing an endowment for the said proposed district a sum of £3,000 : £4 % debenture stock of the North British Railway Company has been purchased and transferred into our name in the books of the said Company by the Revd. John Gorell Haworth, Clerk in Holy Orders . . . of the Vicarge of the new Parish of the Holy Trinity, Tunstead".

70

CHAPTER 7—"OUR WHOAM"

"An Englishman's home is his castle" is an often repeated adage but finding out exactly what this meant for our forefathers in 1846 is almost like travelling with Alice through her looking glass. Try and picture the days before anything was mass-produced or the introduction of any household mechanical device. Even the clock had to be hand-made and clothes were hand-sewn. The 1840's was the last decade of such a life for in the '50's man's ingenuity began to run riot producing every conceivable labour-saving device until today we are immersed in a sea of gadgetry.

The Starkies built in 1717. Notice the peculiar oval windows.

The mediaeval halls and homestead farms were mostly built in stone but there are two interesting domestic brick buildings. The one is the two cottages immediately behind Lower Chesham Hall built in 1713 and the other is what Pevsner calls ". . . . a very curious group of 18th Century "brick houses" called Starkies. The second named were built in 1717 by James Hampson, whose daughter married

Dr. Starkie of Rochdale. Their son was an active supporter of James II, pretender to the throne and during the '45 Jacobite rebellion against the reigning House of Hanover, he trained troops in his home. It was this active rebel who left his name with the houses. When the gable was rebuilt in about 1964 a fascinating embellished stone was reset in its original position ; on it are Hampson's initials, the same date as that on a door lintel and the remnant of a gold-plated coat of arms.

The homes for the industrial workers were much less picturesque than either Chesham or the Starkies. Hoyle's yard, adjacent to the "Weavers' Cottages" built in 1782 was but a foretaste of things to come. Back to back housing in rows in brick or stone became the "jerry-builders'" dream for the cotton operatives and other workers. Even where space was no problem such rows were built, as Red Bank in Bircle, 1833, with communal sanitation and devoid of convenience of any kind except perhaps for a cold water tap. Large families lived in these one-up and one-down homes.

The cottages at Lower Chesham Hall, built 1713.

Cottages on Rochdale Old Road built in 1782.

Stepping through the door into the meagre parlour visitors soon became aware of something old, something new : something borrowed, something blue. Furniture was scarce and very expensive since it was all hand-made. Nothing was thrown away for what Grandma had finished with was passed down to the younger members of the family. Practicality was the fashion and there is little evidence that the influence of men like Robert Adam ever penetrated the harsh realities of northern life. Cottages were roofed with stone slabs or thatch and were not always waterproof hence the value of the canopied four-poster bed, whose side draperies, usually blue gingham, gave some privacy in the family bedroom.

As darkness fell over the moors valley life gradually wound to a halt. Lighting was a scarce commodity in most homes and, before the introduction of paraffin in the 1850's, had to be produced by burning a wick in animal or vegetable oil. If the family were able to afford it tallow candles were burnt, but these cost money and would be the exception rather than the rule. The site now occupied by the "Bury "Times" was once used for the town's tallow candle factory. To avoid wasting money on such luxuries many made do with their own products — a rush dipped again and again in left-over cooking fat. At least this gave free light, the resultant smell was just one of the unfortunate by products.

A typical sheep farmer's moorland home in 1840.

By courtesy of the Castle Folk Museum, York.

Seldom did anyone venture out during the hours of darkness as such escapades were thwarted with danger, both villanous and hazardous with the unlit, unpaved streets. If such a journey was made a "link-boy" was hired as a personal torch bearer who, at least, helped to avoid many pitfalls.

Superstition grew out of expediency. Salt was kept in the rolling pin by the fireplace and was believed to give some protection from evil spirits entering the house and the coloured "witches' ball" hanging in the window was displayed to keep the ladies-on-their-broomsticks at bay. On the floor rushes were thickly strewn to give some insulation against the cold and dampness rising up through the earthern or stone flag floors. Even these poor hovels belonged to the mill-owner and eviction could be at a moment's notice if the employee did not give total satisfaction.

Evening Dress

Day dress for girl

Mill dress—clogs, shawl and apron

Day Dress

The exploitation and the hazards of the workers in Bury helped to provide wealth for England and an opening to world trade which was mainly enjoyed by the south. As people forsook the farm for the factory their hopes were high for an easier and more remunerative life. How soon must their hopes have faded, their faith diminished and their ambitions deflated as, after sixteen hours at the mill, they went "whoam" to rest and recover for six o'clock the next morning when the day's toil began once again its monotonous routine.

The outdoor dress in the mid 1840's
What our ancestors wore in 1846.   Sketches by Mrs. Mildred Denmark.

CHAPTER 8—A FIGHT FOR SURVIVAL

The early days of the nineteenth century may have their romance with the court mannerisms typified by the Minuet amid crinolines and suited gentlemen and with the heroic epics of Wellington defeating Napoleon adding flavour to the glory of English history all seemed well. What was making news in London, however, had no relevance to the events which were changing the face of South-East Lancashire from agricultural hamlets to massive concentrations of factories, mills and houses. Conditions were beyond description and life was cheap, as the workers slaved impossibly long hours over unguarded machinery. The distress between 1837 and 1842 was exceptionally severe. The mills and factories ground to a halt due to a lack of cotton imports restricted by heavy Customs' duties. In many of the towns so many firms had failed that work practically ceased and it is recorded that in Bury, out of 1,157 families, only 1,487 persons had any work to go to, many of these were only partially employed ". . . . and the average amount of weekly earnings per head was found to be only 1s. 9¼d." The Bury Loyal Relief Fund tried to help any family as long as they were not earning more than 2s. 6d. per week. This was the fight for survival.

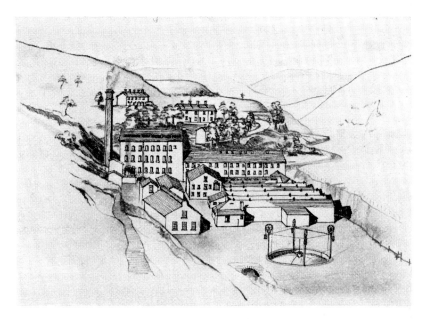

Bircle Dene Mill. A reconstruction by the author.

The Secret Societies

The fight was on and it was by uniting in distress that many rays of hope reached the workers' homes. In secret they banded together and there has been preserved in "Hark to Dangler" on the old coach road north from Bury, the regalia and certificate of the Loyal United Free Mechanics. This Society was formed in 1828 with consent from the Grand Lodge but undoubtedly without the consent of the mill-owners ruling in Birtle Dene and Deeply Vale. These early efforts of Trade-unionism were outlawed and anyone known to be associated with such a movement would be dismissed without any court of appeal.

Mechanics, engineers and operatives gathered in the hostelry from many miles only to return to the appalling conditions at home and work. I am indebted to a thesis in Bury Library "The History of Bury : Lancashire" by Miss Margaret Gray and written in 1965 for information about conditions in the mills, especially one owned by a Thomas Ramsbottom, presumably of Birtle Dene, although Miss Gray does not give us the name of his mill. Wholesale abuse issued from the methods of employment and payment. An entire family would be

The Crimble Beam Engine of James Kenyon. 1827-1925.

on the books of a mill. They probably lived in a mill house for which a deduction of anything up to 6s. 0d. would be made out of a father's maximum wage of £1 10s. 0d. to cover rent, coal and water. A child would receive around 3s. 6d. per week. However it was estimated that the average wage in 1831 of the best workers in the Rochdale mills was around 6s. 0d. per week and Bury would, no doubt, be a parallel.

Mrs. Gaskell wrote her novel "Mary Barton" in 1844 and included the following poem :—

> God help the poor, who in lone valleys dwell,
> Or by far hills, where whim and heather grow !
> Theirs is a story sad indeed to tell ;
> Yet little cares the world, nor seeks to know
> The toil and want poor weavers undergo.
> The irksome loom must have them at morn ;
> They work till worn-out nature will have sleep ;
> They taste, but are not fed.

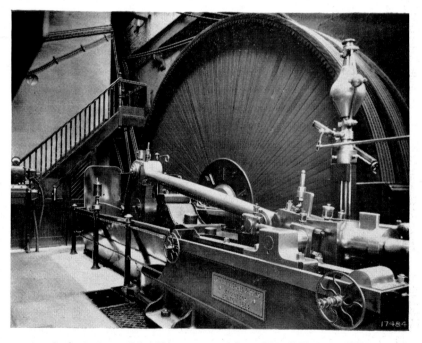

José : built by John Musgrave and Sons Ltd., Bolton, in 1883.

The Mill Engines

The Mechanics and Engineers were not just faced with their human problems but also with the rapid advancement in technology. At first the mills were driven by water-power gathered from the fast flowing streams in the valleys referred to by Mrs. Gaskell. Things soon began to develop out of necessity. The water supply was as spasmodic as the weather and a dry spell of but a few days made a total shut-down inevitable. In 1827 a beam-engine was installed at the Crimble Mill of James Kenyon and such was the workmanship that it continued driving the mill until 1925 — almost a century of vigorous work. One of the famous makers of steam engines was the firm of Musgraves of Bolton and they improved on the design and efficiency to incorporate giant flywheels which became a feature of any engine-room of a cotton mill. At Kenyon's Roach Bank Mill was installed one such engine in 1883 and was named Jose, after Mrs. Kenyon. This did valuable service until 1956 when, like so many others, it gave way to electricity.

The Truck System

Wages were not often paid in money even after 1831 when an Act of Parliament was passed demanding that wages should be made in the coins of the realm. It took nearly forty years for this to become truly effective and an Act in 1887 to stop the loopholes. Disraeli said "this age wants a great deal, but principally wants to have its wages paid in the current coin of the realm". This ideal we enjoy today replaced the Truck System by which a man was compelled to buy his goods at the shop kept either by his employer or by an official of the mill. Some manufacturers went to the trouble to print their own "currency" in the terms of "hours worked". (Such a note for 80 hours work is preserved in the Rochdale Pioneers' Museum), which were only valid in the "Tommy-shop" of the mill.

Nuttall village looking towards the entrance to Nuttall Hall

In Ramsbottom only one mill didn't have a truck-shop and in the village of Nuttall, now completely demolished, there was not one independent shop. A local Chartist, Dr. McDonall, accused owners of overcharging and actually witnessed one man receive the princely sum of 3d. for his week's work, the balance being paid in clothes and other articles. Once a man had got into debt due to high prices for poor quality he became a slave within the system and had a tremendous struggle to get free.

When trade was good, cheap labour became difficult to find so a group of northern industrialists in 1836, including our Thomas Ramsbottom, urged the Poor Law Commissioners to direct labour from the over-populated agricultural lands of the south into the cotton valleys. The first family ever to come north under the scheme came from Sudborne in Suffolk to work in Birtle Dene. Their removal was by cart to London and then to Bury sailing the canal network. An agreement was drawn up for this family by its employer on a three year basis :—

	Age	1st year	WAGES 2nd year	3rd year
SMITH, Jonathan	55	12 0	13 0	14 0
Wife	42			
James		6 0	7 0	8 0
Emma		4 6	5 6	6 6
Sarah....		3 6	4 6	5 6
Jonathan		4 0	5 0	6 0
Ellen		2 6	3 6	4 6
Hannah		—	—	2 6

For this return the family could do anything up to 15 hours work each day beginning at 6-0 a.m. which eventually became curtailed by the famous Ten Hours Bill in 1847. If the manufacturers had kept to their agreement and provided sufficient safeguards for completely unexperienced workers things could have been tolerable, but things went from bad to worse. It is recorded some were soon forced out of work, which also meant eviction from the mill-houses, their only home ; two families suffered smallpox, children were being maimed for life and the degrading proverty was infinitely worse than on the Suffolk farms. The deception which had been practised on these helpless displaced persons by the Manufacturers and the Poor Law Guardians was denounced in an article in "The Times" of 12th May, 1837, which carried the headline "Migration from the Agricultural to the Manufacturing Districts — A Report from Bury in Lancashire". Trade was not just in cotton, it was in the souls of men.

The Co-operative Movement

John Wesley had given one piece of advice to the Wesleyan Society which has since affected the world. He told Christians to help "each other in business — and so much the more because the world will love its own, and them only". Before 1844 attempts were made to put these words into practice but the one which finally won the approval and confidence of men was in Rochdale with the formation of the

The shop front of 31 Toad Lane, Rochdale

Pioneers' Society. It was the overwhelming difficulties which drew together men of different political and religious persuasions. Some movers in the early Co-op. Movement were ensnared in the Truck System but supported their own shop whilst freeing themselves. The human story of how 28 men collected total assets of £28 at the rate of 2d. per week from their members and took the tremendous step of

Model of the interior of the Rochdale Pioneers

faith to rent the ground floor of a warehouse for three years at £10 per annum reflects the desperation of their plight. Eventually the first Co-op. shop was opened on 21st December, 1844, at 31 Toad Lane, Rochdale. The pioneers had spent a total of £16 11s. 11d. on their stock — 1 qr. 22 lbs. of butter ; 2 qrs. sugar ; 3 sacks at 37s. 6d. and 3 at 36s. 0d. of flour ; 1 sack of oatmeal and 2 dozen candles. The sales staff totalled two men paid 3d. per hour. That first shop has been preserved as a museum of the Co-operative Movement and it is with gratitude I include the pictures.

Bury had an early experiment that failed. In 1850, a Society was formed under the name of "The General Labour Redemption Society" and they opened a shop on 20th October, 1851, at No. 50 Stanley Street (now a section of The Rock). In a total period of eighteen months it had flourished to a membership of over 500 with a turnover of £50 per week and died due to a lack of efficient accountancy and mistrust. The total trade was about £1,660 before it was finally wound up on 3rd April, 1853.

No. 50 Stanley Street

From the ashes of failure was to rise a monument of success in Bury. In 1855 a group of ten men held regular meetings in the greenhouse of a Heywood Street home belonging to Mr. Richard Sully. They were encouraged by the success of the Rochdale Pioneers' and reports of similar ventures in Lancashire towns so putting behind them the failure of the General Labour Redemption Society they formed the "Bury District Co-operative Society". The first members paid 3d. per week to form the necessary capital which amounted to £6 9s. 6d. by the end of the year. The sole trading was one load of flour which had cost £2 5s. 9d. One of the pillars of the Pioneers was that membership was opened to people of various religious and political persuasions, so long as they were willing to co-operate, a principle adopted in Bury in these early days. Fortunately help and "know-how" came from a Halifax business-man, Mr. Smithson, and it was largely due to his support that a shop at No. 11 Market Street was taken on an agreed annual rent of £31, the first payment being made on 26th April, 1856. Mr. Smithson had offered to supply goods on condition he was paid once they had been sold and it is some testimony to his co-operation that he waited nearly a whole year before receiving his first payment. At first the shop was staffed by its own members during the evening hours of 6 p.m. to 10 p.m. and no credit was allowed.

In August, 1856 the next step was taken and that was to pay a dividend from the profits. The wise-men of Bury consulted with their Rochdale counterparts and then shared out a total of £18 0s. 2d. In the same month the Committee was compelled to consider changing from evening selling to opening the shop all day, employing a shop-keeper and assistant (their salaries were 20s. 0d. and 4s. 0d. per week). An advertisement appeared in the "Bury Times" for 30th August, 1856 that "The public will be supplied with articles of the best quality at the most reasonable prices". Trading times were given as "Daily 8 till half-past 9. Saturday till 11".

The birth pangs of Bury Co-op. had been difficult and their delegates to the Conference on Christmas Day, 1862, called to discuss establishing the Co-operative Wholesale Society, recommended their members not to join the scheme. Other Societies went ahead and began their combined Wholesale Society in 1863, but it was not until 1887 that the Bury Movement associated itself with it.

The early Co-operators were determined not just to clothe and feed themselves but were bent on better housing at a reasonable cost. In 1867 it was resolved that some portion of the Society's capital be used for building "cottages". Authority was given to the Committee of Management to build up to sixty dwellings. The first lot was a block of ten in Shepherd Street, immediately followed by sixteen in Raven Street. Since then many of the members utilised the Society as a Building Society and purchased their homes. By this time the fight for survival was over, circumstances had so altered that the workers and employers were no longer bound together and a new era was to build up the Industrial prosperity of Bury.

Money Matters

One of the greatest aids to allow the work folk to grow independent and own their own houses was the establishing of Savings Banks up and down the land. Daniel Defoe, the author of "Robinson Crusoe" urged for the foundation of such banks in an essay which he wrote in 1698 as a means of encouraging thrift and perhaps helping to solve his financial problem of £17,000. The first such bank was at Wendover, in the South country, started by the Rev. Joseph Smith in 1799 as a Parish Bank. Others followed suit and brought pressure to bear when

Raven Street

Pitt, the Prime Minister, thought that the remedy for widespread poverty was to provide every respectable pauper with a cow.

Small individual Banks were being set up when the Savings Bank Act of 1817 regularised their dealings and popularised the movement. Five years later, March 1822 "The Bury Bank for Savings" was inaugurated on the site occupied today by Martins Bank in Silver Street and was open for business from 6 p.m. till 8 p.m. each Saturday evening. The first President was the Rev. Geoffrey Hornby and such familiar names as Robinson Kay, Grant and Wrigley appear on the lists of former trustees. The first depositor, called John Moore, invested thirty shillings to open his account which was short-lived as soon after he withdrew the whole amount.

In 1850, out of the accumulated surplus, a new building was erected on the opposite corner of Bank Street and Silver Street. A clock which is still in possession of the bank, was made to order by a Bury clock-maker, Mr. Croasdale. By the middle of the 1960's the now "Trustee Savings Bank" had nearly sixty-four and a half thousand subscribers and the old premises unable to cope with such an increased clientele. On Thursday, 1st September, 1966, a new Head Office, designed by Bury Architects : Richard Byrom, Hill & Partners, was officially opened to facilitate the custodianship of funds totalling over £13 million. Hard won prosperity has brought much for the people.

Interior of Trustee Savings Bank

CHAPTER 9—
"FROM ME TO YOU WITH LOVE" — THE POST OFFICE

Letters are one of today's enjoyable means of communicating with our friends and families. We take for granted the daily post on our breakfast table and perhaps find some interest in the stamp on the envelope which may be a new "commemorative". In 1846 the arrival of a letter would have been a major event in a cotton worker's home and many of the operatives would take it to the Vicar, or some professional letter-writer to have it read.

In 1801 a Sub-Post Office was established in Bury and a Mrs. Cooper appointed to be in charge on the recommendations of Sir Robert Peel. Where exactly Mrs. Cooper had her office is in question. One source of information suggests it was in Broad Street on the site of the present N.W. Gas Board Showrooms whereas an early map of Bury shows it a few yards down Bury Lane (now Bolton Street) from Silver Street. If the map is anything to go by it was a very small office and within easy reach of the two coaching inns in the Market Place.

Post Offices in those days were little more than receiving kiosks. The famous "penny black", the first stick on postage stamp in the world, was not introduced until 6th May, 1840. If you wrote a letter before that date and wished for it to be taken by the Royal Mail then you would take it and leave it at the Post Office who charged the recipient on a so-much-per-sheet basis on delivery. Pillar-boxes did not come into fashion until after 1852 but to make posting a little easier in some towns and cities, a letter-carrier walked through the streets after the office had closed, ringing a bell calling attention for people to "post" their letters in the carrier's bag — the nearest thing to a walking postbox.

The sending of money has always been a postal problem. Various kinds of ingenious safeguards were made by the sender to try and ensure their money's safe arrival. Sometimes "notes" were cut in half by peculiar zig-zag lines and the two halves sent separately by post and then matched by the receiver. The one snag with this was that if one half failed to arrive the only satisfaction was of knowing that the thief was no better off. In 1792 the Post Office introduced a money-order service with a charge of 6d. in £1 and a maximum of £5 5s. 0d. but it was not until 1856 that the Bury Post Office was granted the status of a "Money Order Office".

It is hardly credible that a major event in 1854 was the appointment of a third letter-carrier, which enabled an extension of the delivery area. In 1859 the three "postmen" were given new uniforms reflecting the importance of their office. For fine weather it was scarlet topped with the glory of cockades with kits of oilskins for the familiar rainy day.

Compulsory education was finally introduced into England in 1870 which brought a tremendous upsurge in the postage of letters. To make way for this and to deal with the revival in trade after the 1860s' cotton famine two "town receiving offices" were added to the postal

One of the first Pallar Boxes, 1856-1860
Photo by courtesy of H.M. Postmaster General.

facilities : one at Moorgate and the other at Bury Bridge. The demand on the Service continued to grow and it was found the original Post Office could not cater for the needs of the town it served. In 1872 it was rebuilt and this may have been the time when it moved to Broad Street away from the environment of the Market Place and its coaching inns. The picturesque stage-coach era lasted from 1784 to the early 1840's, when the railway replaced the horse drawn mail coaches. In an age when we have grown accustomed to multi-methods of transport it is difficult to conceive the full impact of the steam train after thousands of years of horse-power. To some extent the history of the Post Office is a reflection of transport development as each subsequent improvement was utilised to speed the Royal Mail. There was a reversal of this principle in 1887 when the charges made by the Railway Companies became so excessive that the Post Office brought the stage-coaches out of storage and there was a short-lived revival of the "Wells-Fargo" glory. Steam-powered vans : motor vehicles and bicycles have all played their part.

The Mail Coach Revival.   London-Oxford, 1890.
By courtesy of H.M. Postmaster General.

Telegrams were not unknown in 1846 although very expensive. The first telegram instrument was on trial in 1837 between two London Railway Stations, Euston and Campden Town. Two years later a permanent service was set up between the Metropolis and Slough but it was well into the 1850's before the system became widely established.

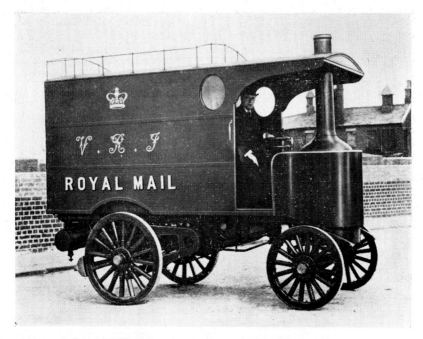

A Royal Mail Steam Van of 1901
By courtesy of British Leyland Motors Ltd.

Few developments took place from then until the 1920's. Samuel Morse had provided his famous "code" for the early telegraphic system but this was replaced on inland services by the teleprinter which is most famous for providing football fans with the scores on Saturday afternoon television.

A much later invention than telegrams was the telephone. Although many Victorian stage plays have some antique looking receivers they were comparatively rare before this century. Graham Bell first demonstrated the practical telephone to Queen Victoria at Osborne House on the Isle of Wight in 1878 and in the following year the first telephone services were established.

Two facts from 1900 conclude our short excursion into the Post Office world of 125 years ago. The one of major importance is that it was in the first year of this century that the Bury Post Office moved into its present home in Crompton Street. That same year Mrs. Greenhalgh opened Jericho Sub-Post Office with an aim — £5 worth of business per week.

The solitary isolation of the mills in the valleys is no figment of the imagination when the primitive state of the postal service without telegrams or telephones is realised and so it is not to be wondered at how the mill owners could keep the employees in a kingdom of their design.

THIS SKETCH

is respectfully dedicated to the

UNIVERSITY OF OXFORD.

Published by J.Dickinson New Bond Street

Printed by C.Hullmandel

Sir Robert Peel speaking in the House of Commons
By courtesy of Borough Librarian.

CHARLEYS AND BOBBIES

"Two o'clock and all's well" is a well known cry from the village watchman as he made the half-hourly round of his "beat". These Charleys, as they were affectionately called, were self-appointed volunteers and acted in partnership with the Parish Constable. The office of Constable had been given official recognition towards the end of the fourteenth century and the appointment was subject to the annual Vestry Meeting. Things were far from satisfactory. The often old and decrepit Charley, weighed down with his heavy overcoat, shoulder capes and carrying his large horn lantern was no protection for the sleeping community whilst the corrupt and drunken constables often created more crime than they solved. In the reign of King James I (1603-1625) it is known that these "law-enforcement officers" gathered a living by basket-justice, so called because of the empty baskets which they displayed to receive gifts from petitioners and offenders. It was just this sort of racket which brought the name of Constable into disrepute and considerable pressure built up in the eighteenth century to establish an organised Police Force. A man called Patrick Colquhoun proposed, in effect, what Robert Peel was forced to create a generation later.

Following the Napoleonic Wars many ex-soldiers and unemployed men turned their hand to crime, and to make some attempt to curtail these criminals in London, Sir Robert Peel, during his spell as Home Secretary, introduced the Metropolitan Police Act in 1829 and was supported by the Duke of Wellington, the Prime Minister. The speed and effect of their action was startling. The Bill was presented to the House of Commons on 15th April and it received Royal Assent on 19th July of that same year. The principle of a Police Force established although the Act had no power to help the industrial areas with their problems of inadequate housing, drunkenness and unemployment amongst the people who left their peaceful village homes for a life in the mill towns. A further Police Act was passed in 1839 requiring magistrates to set up Forces in their counties and a later Bill (1856) laid the same responsibilities on the magistrates of the large towns and cities.

Bury came under the Lancashire County Constabulary and it is the only County Borough in England which continued under a County's jurisdiction. One reason may have been that in 1839 a Police Station was opened in Agur Street and the following year policemen in their uniform of top hat and white trousers began to patrol the streets. The Bury Station was under the supervision of Lancashire's Chief Constable, John Woodford, who was elected by the magistrates as head of the 500 strong force. As first Cheif Constable he had the responsibility of organising his men into some sort of order so he first visited London to see the Metropolitan Force at work and gathered what material he could from it.

Woodford divided the work up into the fifteen divisions corresponding to the Petty Sessional divisions of the County. Order, however, gained neither respect nor popularity. The Constable had cost a

The Market Place, Bury, dominated by the statue of Sir Robert Peel complete with his waistcoat buttons on the wrong side.

Parish about £100 per annum but the "Bobbies" or "Peelers" so named after Robert Peel were now costing nearly £900. The opposition grew to such a level that in 1841 the magistrates voted that ". . . . the police force should be abolished on the grounds of uselessness and expense". Although the motion was carried the majority was insufficient under the County Police Act for its dissolution but drastic reductions had to be made in man-power. The new force was to consist of 355 Constables employed at a pay of 18s. 0d. per week.

Drunkenness was as common amongst the police as elsewhere in the 1840's. These were the days before the introduction of licensing hours and liquor flowed cheap in the multitude of brew-houses at any hour of day or night. Of the first 200 men to be appointed 50 were dismissed for being drunk within six months of their appointment and

Police uniforms, as they were when the Force was formed, and as they are today.

one man who had his services dispensed with for the offence was finally transported to serve seven years for bigamy. It is difficult to realise that legislation protecting life and property was not enacted until the numerous penal acts of 1861 when such Acts as the Offences against the Person, the Larceny, and the Malicious Damage was enforced by Parliament.

The Uniform in 1911

The Tenterden Street Police Station, 1928-1970

In 1850 the home of Bury's Police moved into the new Civic Buildings on Market Street which included the Derby Hotel and Town Hall. The Constabulary was gaining respect from the public and confidence in itself. The changing face was reflected in its uniform. The first regulation was made in 1848 with the introduction of the frock-coat and a cap to replace the top hat. Not every division accepted H.Q. decisions and it was Chief Constable Moorsom in 1897 who finally ordered that top hats must not be worn as they were an outmoded part of any uniform. Long before Moorsom's prohibition on top hats, the familiar helmet had been introduced. In 1864 a wide sweeping experiment took place which included the helmet and a change of colour to green. The colour was short-lived and the value of the traditional Bobbies' "blue" soon recognised but the helmet has withstood the fashions down the years and is still to be seen in the streets. In 1935 the Home Office standardised Police uniform ; so ended the individuality of each force.

Police duties have not altered. The four tasks set before them are : the preservation of life and property : the prevention and detection of crime : the maintenance of order and the prosecution of offenders against the peace. In order to fulfil their appointed roll for Bury a completely new building was opened in 1928 on Tenterden Street and in 1970 another Headquarters has been opened to facilitate the large area committed to this Division following certain boundary revisions.

It seems a far cry from the three Constables appointed by Lord Derby's court-leet in the old fortified Manor House to the highly respected Police force today operating from their five-storeyed modern H.Q. This revolution is another example of the changing pattern of life as the industrial society developed.

JAMES GREENWOOD
LTD.

BUILDING CONTRACTORS

HUNTLEY BROOK
BURY BL9 7PR

Tel. 061-764 2203-4

CHAPTER 11—BURY CHAPEL

There are times when the character of a nation receives an indelible mark from events which happen in a single generation — sometimes for good, others for ill. One crowning piece of folly for England, and especially for Lancashire, was the return of the gay Cavalier, King Charles II, and his imposition of the Act of Uniformity in A.D. 1662. The hundred years preceding this could be termed "the reign of the Puritans" when a deep sincere Christian religion pervaded the length and breadth of the country. It was the clash between the followers of the Puritans and the sympathisers of the High Anglican party which brought about the tragic events of the Civil War. The country revolted against the religious antics of Archbishop Laud and Charles I and for ten years the Presbyterian form of Government held sway under the reins of Oliver Cromwell.

A whole chapter could be written on the pros and cons of those sad years and a good case made out to gain sympathy for both sides. Leaving aside all the intrigues and personalities involved it must be remembered that politics and religion were so inter-woven it is difficult to differentiate one from the other. To help provide for the spiritual needs of the people the Commonwealth had appointed only Ministers who upheld the Christian way of life and preached with sincere Biblical Authority. Lancashire was divided into nine Presbyteries, the second of which included the Parishes of Bolton, Bury, Middleton, Rochdale, Deane and Radcliffe. In the 1650 Survey the clergy who served the Presbytery are described as mostly "godly preaching ministers . . . . of good life and conversation". These men were renowned for their personal sincerity and Mr. Schofield of Heywood was said to be "orthodox for divinity and well qualified for life", whilst the then Rector of Bury was to suffer eviction as being unacceptable to the Elders.

In 1662 the Act of Uniformity was inflicted upon the country by the wilful deceit of Charles II aided by Archbishop Sheldon. Any religious exercise by more than five people was forbidden except by using the Book of Common Prayer. Rather than accept this ridiculous imposition, which made some Christian families refrain from saying Grace before meals, 2,000 clergy resigned their livings and of these 67 ministered in Lancashire — three in the Ancient Parish of Bury, George Thomason of Heywood, Henry Pendlebury of Holcombe and the Rector, John Lightfoot. It was senseless fanaticism which banished these men from their Ministries whilst other men, many of whom were famed for bear-baiting, cock-fighting and drinking bouts, could continue in their livings so long as they conformed to the letter of the Prayer Book.

One Ejected Minister

The Rev. Henry Pendlebury was born at Jowkin Farm, near Bamford Hall, on 6th May, 1626. His early education was at "Bury Grammar School" whatever form this took at that time. He entered Christ Church, Cambridge, as an under-graduate where he obtained his M.A. in 1648. In his year of graduation he preached his first sermon in Ashworth Chapel, near to his birth-place, and was "ordained" in 1650 in Turton Chapel. For the next twelve months he ministered at Horwich Chapel in the Parish of Deane and on 16th October, 1651, was inducted to Holcombe, where he fulfilled a worthy Ministry for eleven years.

Jowkin Farm, Bamford.

Bury's first Non-Conformist Chapel, Bass Lane.

Many of those ejected Ministers were deeply conscious of their Christ-given commission to preach the Holy Scriptures and care for the Christians committed to their charge, so being deprived of their temporal livings they continued to labour where and how they could. It is recorded by Baines in his History of Lancashire (1868) that there was a "Presbyterian Chapel at Bass Lane, Walmersley, built in 1664 and rebuilt in 1797, now a farm house. Tradition identifies Bass House as the spot where Henry Pendlebury settled with his wife after leaving Holcombe and established the first Non-Conforming Meeting House in Bury. He left in his Will the sum of 40s. 0d. a year ". . . . . to such Minister as shall officiate at the said Chapell . . . . and that the said chapell may only be used for the public worship of God and for no other purpose". What exactly became of the building is subject to speculation for it was once recorded as having "gone to ruin and decay", whilst the building in the centre of the Bass House group is named "The Chapel House". The present Bass Lane leading from Walmersley Road to Cragg Farm is misnamed for originally the road was on the other side of the main road leading across the fields to the old coach road via Bass House.

The ejected Ministers were followed by many of their congregations and it is a testimony to the effectiveness of Pendlebury's Ministry that the Church he planted, under God, is still in existence, represented by Bank Street Unitarian Chapel. On 18th June, 1695, after 45 years of Ministry, thirty-three of which were spent preaching where he could and was allowed, he was buried "close by the chancel wall on the south-side" of Bury Parish Church. A small brass plaque in the floor records him as "Henry Pendlebury : A faithful Minister of the Gospel". On

9th May, 1714 was held the last recorded service in Bass Lane, which had lost many of its adherents to Dundee Chapel at Holcombe which had opened on 5th August, 1712, through a certificate of toleration issued by the Archdeacon of Chester. In five years the congregation had grown to nearly 600 and in 1719 a Presbyterian Meeting House was built in Bury on the corner of Bank Street and Silver Street. By the mid-nineteenth century this place was the centre of the most influential congregation in the town and gave a noble lead in the relief of hunger and poverty, whilst campaigning for temperance and other reforms.

"Into Bury"

In 1832 there came to "Bury Chapel" (so called as initially the only other place of worship in the town was "Bury Church") the Rev. Franklin Howorth. Franklin's early life was spent in Audenshaw, near Manchester, and he was educated at the Boys' School of the Fairfield Moravian Church, Droylsden. No doubt it was the instruction he received at this school which was to bring such an influence into Bury.

The Old Chapel, once described as "the quaint old ivy-covered chapel with its V front" had veered from its Puritan foundation to embrace the Unitarian form of doctrine and the Rev. Franklin Howorth was called to continue in this new position. He was a talented preacher and the congregation grew so quickly that after two years it was resolved to build a larger Chapel. In 1837 this new Chapel was opened for worship and it was whilst ministering in the new "Bank Street Presbyterian Chapel" that Mr. Howorth moved away from Unitarianism to the Christian faith and he was often to be found in a Methodist Prayer Meeting or joining in fellowship with the Primitive Methodists, or Ranters. Although protests against his Gospel preaching grew amongst the "orthodox Unitarians" he remained at Bank Street for 22 years. Finally on 29th July, 1853, he wrote to his congregation resigning from his Pastorate signing himself "Ever your friend and brother in Christ". At this moment Franklin Howorth forfeited the most influential position in Bury — the pulpit of "Bury Chapel".

The second Chapel built in 1837 had only a short life of about 15 years. Adjacent to the West Wall of the building the East Lancashire Railway Company made a deep cutting to allow for the building of their Bolton Street Station. The Chapel was badly affected by ensuing earth movement and ultimately another one had to be built. The replacement was erected on the same site at the rear of the burial ground and was in regular use until May, 1970, when it finally closed its doors to be replaced by a new Chapel providing for the needs of the congregation in the second-half of the 20th Century. The estimated cost of the new building is £60,000 which would have increased by another third if it had been built over the foundations of its two predecessors. Mr. J. T. Radcliffe of Bury is the Architect of the imaginative scheme. "Bank Street" has a record of fine music and the fine three manual organ which was in the third Chapel is to be dismantled and provide some ranks of pipe for the new instrument.

Bank Street Chapel from Silver Street

Photo : "Bury Times".

The Chapel at Holebottom

The wealthy congregation of the last century also provided for themselves a second burial ground at Holebottom. The Chapel once owned considerable lands east of Bury, one section was utilized for the cemetery and another part was sold to Bury Corporation for part of a post-war housing scheme. In the centre of the graveyard stands a small neo-Gothic Chapel which was once furnished with pews to seat the mourners at a funeral and the congregation for the annual "Memorial Service". Few burials take place at Holebottom in the 1970's and the Chapel is used as the grave-digger's tool shed, subject to continual vandalism and awaiting the congregation's final decision upon its fate.

Interior of Bank Street Chapel, demolished 1970.

Christian Church

The Ministry of the Rev. Franklin Howorth did not stop in 1853 on his resignation from the pastorate of Bank Street. On 13th August, 1854, he announced the opening of a new Christian Meeting House in Commercial Buildings, Spring Street, welcoming all ". . . . who love the Lord Jesus in sincerity and are willing to work in His Service". Howorth, at his own expense, had transformed the Concert Hall of the Commercial Hotel into a Church and Sunday School. His congregation contained both old friends from Bank Street and members he had drawn through his pastoral visiting in the vicinity.

The new congregation were not to remain in their Music Hall for long and on 10th July, 1859, the foundation stone of "Christian Church" on Rochdale Road was laid and the Chapel opened in September of the following year. 1860 saw a further expansion of the Rev. F. Howorth's Ministry when he was involved, with three laymen, in founding "The Bury Sunday Evening Ragged School" in the Bolton Street shop of Thomas Pennington, chemist. In 1869 this School moved to new premises in George Street to serve a desperately needy generation. This ex-Bank Street Minister was also responsible for bringing the Y.M.C.A. movement into Bury and was the first President until his death on 12th June, 1882, at the age of seventy-seven. The Rev. Franklin Howorth was buried in Bury Cemetery after working for fifty years in the town and the list of mourners at the funeral service bears testimony to the impact this man had on his generation.

CHAPTER 11—THIS PART OF WESLEY'S PARISH

As the spiritual fervour of the Puritan followers died in succeeding generations, a spiritual and moral decay descended over the land as parsons came to be noted as "four or five bottle men" — the title was determined by the number of bottles of port they could drink at one sitting. A group of Oxford undergraduates formed their Holy Club and amongst its members was John Wesley who was ordained into the Church of England. For ten years Wesley ministered in vain both in England and on the other side of the Atlantic in Georgia. On 24th May, 1738, at a meeting of the Moravian Church in Aldersgate, London, Wesley said "I felt my heart strangely warmed. I felt I did trust in Christ, Christ alone for salvation, and an assurance was given me . . . . and I then testified openly to all".

The visits of the Preacher

With the world as his Parish, Wesley travelled the length and breadth of England preaching that vital faith he had experienced in London. In places where he visited or where his co-workers went many people found their spiritual needs met in Christ. A spiritual awaking moved through the town of Bolton and many Bury inhabitants were seen making their way along Bolton Road. From these travellers sprang up the first Methodist Meeting House at Pits o'th' Moor in Bury. The property was vested in the name of the Rev. John Wesley and co-trustees so that when a larger building was needed, a personal request had to be made to the itinerant preacher for permission to sell the existing premises. Sanction was given by a letter to Mr. James Hall.

The building of the second Chapel at Pits o'th' Moor reveals a pathetic picture. Due to religious intolerance no local firm would supply any building material so the Methodists simply had to make their own. In his "Life of Wesley" the Rev. L. Tyreman describes the scene "At Bury, Methodism had been cradled in a storm. On some occasions the people were besmeared with the most offensive filth, and Services were disturbed by the blowing of huntsmen's horns again and again. These poor Methodists dug up the clay and burnt the bricks. Some worked by day, others by night".

The new Chapel was opened on Saturday, 16th April, 1774, by the Rev. John Wesley himself, who wrote in his Journal "I preached at a preaching house just built at Chowbent, which was lately a den of lions ; but now they are lambs. So they were the next day at the new house near Bury". This was not the only time he visited the town for other references are dated Wednesday, 17th April, 1776 ; Friday, 26th July, 1778; Monday, 12th April, 1779; Thursday, 6th April, 1780 and a Friday, in April, 1787. Of this last visit he wrote ". . . . . I was invited to breakfast at Bury by Mr. Peel, a calico printer, who, a few years ago began with five hundred pounds and is now supposed to have gained some fifty thousand pounds. O what a miracle if he lose not his soul".

Union Street Chapel, 1815-1969.   Interior and Exterior.

Apparently the great Evangelist found no friendship with the Rev. and Hon. Stanley but was asked ". . . . after dinner by the Rev. James Hargreaves . . . . if he would play a game at cards". Mr. Wesley refused, bid farewell to Mr. Peel and the company "rode from Chamber Hall and left Bury" to continue the more worthy occupation of preaching.

Clerke Street Sunday School. Demolished 1970.

Union Street Chapel

As the Methodist congregation increased it became obvious a town-centre meeting-place was an essential. The first such Chapel was in Clerke Street which incorporated a Sunday School from some "long room" in Cross Street. The son of a Mr. and Mrs. Sutcliffe who had his first lessons in the Clerke Street School was later appointed Governor of the Island of Juan Fernandez in 1835 and published an authoritative work on the government and geography of the island. The Clerke Street premises continued in use as a Sunday School, after such minor alterations as removing pews, until 1968 when they were purchased for the redevelopment schemes. The premises, however, had played but a secondary roll after the Union Street Chapel was built in 1815.

The Union Street Chapel, which still stands after a thorough modernisation scheme in 1969, was the result of one man seeking to serve the Lord with the same vision and zeal of Wesley. In 1804 Bury became the centre of the Bury, Heywood and Radcliffe circuit, whose first steward was Mr. James Wrigley, of a different family from the Wrigleys of Bridge Hall. James was born at Chesham to parents who regularly attended the Parish Church. He became a scholar at the Free School in Stanley Street but his academic career was short-lived and he was apprenticed ". . . . as a woollen weaver, and threw the shuttle for many years in Bury and at Walmersley". At the age of eighteen James married and found the wolf of poverty ever at his door with the responsibilities of a large family. In consequence of a dream, trouble commenced which terminated in his conversion to God. His dream related to the strait gate and the narrow way . . . he was so affected that he rose at four o'clock one morning to find the Scripture account". His thoughts often caught up with his circumstances for each day he half expected having bailiffs to sell what goods he and his wife owned to pay their cottage rent of £2 each half-year. He was dismissed from Sunday School for lack of attendance and was either sacked, or left Kay's at Bass Lane. The night he became unemployed he went to Chamber Hall and, having met Robert Peel senior at the entrance, managed to borrow £5 for three months to start dealing in waste material. The money was returned on the appointed day and he obtained a double loan for six months. At the end of the agreed period James Wrigley again returned to Chamber Hall to repay the loan and came away with £20 to be repaid when he could. Wrigley bought the Gigg Estate and established a bleach works. He became a close friend of his benefactor who once confided to him "would to God I had never known greatness".

As Wrigley prospered so he honoured the Lord with his substance. In the 1810's he began looking for the site on which to build the new Methodist Chapel and he managed to acquire the land in two separate transactions, one costing £427 and the other £200. He then opened a subscription list to build the new Chapel and began with a donation of £300 and obtained a 100 gns. from his son. The Chapel was opened in 1815 and consecrated in 1817 but Mr. Wrigley was only satisfied with the best possible for His Lord's Worship, so he sought support to erect an organ in the Chapel. The instrument cost £250 of which he subscribed £223.

A note worth recording written in 1890 reveals what values were placed on spiritual things by early Methodists ". . . . if a collection at a Sunday School reached the 'teens of pounds it was considered marvellous (this was in the hungry '40's) now £60, £80 or even £100 are not considered more than satisfactory".

108

The redesigned Chapel

Photo : C. M. Cleworth.

The Union Street Chapel stood unaltered for over 150 years. The last Service was the Harvest Thanksgiving in 1968. Once closed the interior was literally gutted, including the gallery, and a scheme designed by Richard Byrom, Hill & Partners, Architects, put into practice. In place of the one huge auditorium and two small vestries there is now a Chapel to seat about 250 people, a large hall and four classrooms. This fine modernised Church unit was re-opened by the Secretary of the Methodist Conference, Dr. Eric W. Baker, on Saturday, 3rd January, 1970, and used for worship the following day. The sale of the Clerke Street premises bore about half the cost and a generous grant from the Joseph A. Rank Benevolent Trust helped considerably. Two near-centre-town Chapels, Parkhills and Heywood Street were closed and joined with Union Street. The present congregation are utilising the new facilities and one community service is the provision of coffee for shoppers on Market Days.

In the 1800's many Methodist Chapels were opened to serve the spiritual needs of many people. The first "daughter" of Union Street was Moulding Chapel in Bircle, opened on 14th March, 1824, which, like the Pits o'th' Moor Second Chapel, was a do-it-yourself-through-opposition building. A Bible Study, Prayer Group had been meeting regularly in a nearby farm and this formed the nucleus of the congregation. The Chapel had been standing for twenty-two years before Bircle Parish Church was consecrated.

Interior of Brunswick Chapel: A sketch by kind permission of Mr. G. E. T. Franklin.

From the hill country. Holcombe with the Peel Monument in the background.

1834 Secession

Once the founder, under God, of Methodism had died many fermenting problems began to erupt. One dispute for discussion at the 1834 Conference was the proposal to establish Theological training colleges. To many this was abhorrent as it cast a suspicion on the worthiness of the lay-preachers. Not just the idea brought bitter opposition but the "politics" of introducing the scheme went awry. Following this Conference the "Grand Central Association" was formed to try and modify the decisions of the parent body but without success and so formed the distinctive organisation known as the "Wesleyan Methodists".

Dissent was first stirred in Bury at a meeting on 10th April, 1835, by a group of men who were deeply committed to retaining unaltered Wesley's scheme. John Robinson Kay was duly expelled from the Bury circuit by the Superintendent Minister for his sympathies, others left of their own accord. On an unrecorded date in the late Autumn 1835 "One Sunday morning, the scholars and teachers assembled in Clerke Street School, according to custom. The hour at length arrived for adjournment to the Chapel in Union Street for Divine Worship. The procession, however, took a different direction. Some few elected to go to the Chapel as usual, but the large majority proceeded along Clough Street, Stanley Street, and John Street and finally entered a building that had been used as a woollen warehouse belonging to Messrs. Harrison in Paradise Street where a room had been made ready. The number in that procession is quite incredible — 176 teachers and 863 scholars".

This room in the warehouse became affectionately known as "The Tabernacle" but on the annual Sermons Day the congregation had to move to the warehouse itself, capable of seating 3,000. It became tradition in the Evening Service to sing Handel's Hallelujah Chorus and on one occasion it is reported the Leader of the Orchestra was seen waving his violin bow over his head, because, he confessed afterwards, ". . . . it went so well". On Whit-Friday, 27th May, 1836, the foundation stone was laid for the first Brunswick Chapel, which was later used as the school. During the night vandals removed the stone and stole the entombed articles. Work proceeded and the Chapel was opened on 24th March (Good Friday), 1837. Brunswick prospered under the Ministry of men like William Stott who gave up his mechanics career to become the first Missioner at the salary of £1 per week. In 1861 the Society began to build a new Chapel with a balance of £3,000 already in the bank and it was opened for worship on Wednesday, 7th December, 1864, which must have been quite a tonic for the town in the cotton famine. Like Union Street, Brunswick became the centre of its own circuit and Churches at Heap Bridge (1837), Limefield (1849), Elton (1858), Bircle (1862) and Parkhills (1881) amongst others were established.

After 100 years Brunswick's doors shut for the last time and the building was demolished in preparation for the inner ring road. The story of this part of Wesley's Parish is of men who cared deeply for the things of the Lord Jesus Christ and who, in their day, promoted true religion. Unfortunately they left a legacy of enormous premises which have been beyond the financial resources of their successors but this in no way diminishes the contribution they made to the life of the town and the ancient Parish of Bury.

CHAPTER 13—PLEASE TEACHER!

The Wedding Registers of any Parish in the industrial belt of Lancashire tell a sad tale from the 1800's. Numerous entries are found where a man or his bride have had to place a cross, instead of signing their name, and the Minister signed it for them with the words "his mark". It was not through wilful neglect that people could not write. School attendance was voluntary until 1876 and before that time children, sometimes as young as seven, could find employment in the mills. Education was scarce, a luxury few could afford and most felt unjustified in letting their children spend time learning instead of earning.

The Grammar School

The beginning of many schools is shrouded in legend and often individual efforts. There were always those who pinned their hopes on education and there is a reference to a man who attended school under a Mr. Johnson in Bury, dated 1617. Another birth-date is given by Hulme Elliot who says that Bury Grammar School was founded in 1625. One-teacher-schools sprang up where there was a demand for them and since only scanty records were made the remaining evidence is often just a name. There is, however, documentary evidence of some educational establishment in Bury in 1634 when the Rev. Henry Bury bequeathed £300 to "the school in Bury". The benefactor was at Manchester Grammar School and through his generosity showed confidence in the Head Master, the Rev. Henry Dunster to build a worthwhile school. Beginning with Mr. Dunster there is a fairly complete list of Head Masters of the School which has evolved into Bury Grammar School for Boys.

Portrait of the Rev. Roger Kay from Bury Grammar School for Girls
By kind permission of the Headmistress

The Rev. Henry Pendlebury was just one of the students who went on to Cambridge or Oxford from Bury School in the 17th Century. Unfortunately the bequest of £300 became quite insufficient to maintain and expand the work and it was another Bury-exile, remembering his home town, who revitalised the school nearly one hundred years later. In 1726 the Rev. Roger Kay, M.A., assigned land to re-establish a "schole for teaching grammar in Bury". Kay was born at Woodhill in 1663 and was himself educated at Bury School before going to St. John's College, Cambridge, where he graduated and became a Fellow. He was appointed to the Rectory of Fittleton in the Diocese of Salisbury and became a Prebendary of that See. In his will he directed that the 6th May be "Visitation Day" when the Trustees shall meet and a Sermon preached in the Parish Church on "the usefulness of public benefactions of this nature, as a means to induce and move others to add to this, my charity".

The Rev. Roger Kay also left a sum of £5 yearly in order that ten poor girls born, or to be born, in the Parish and town of Bury, might receive an education "to make them perfect in their Reading the Bible, to teach 'em to write well, and to be good Accountants to fit 'em for Trades or to be good Servants". They were to be examined by the Rector "as a Trustee and Governor of the free Grammar Scholl of Bury". This foundation never materialised for education in Kay's time was chiefly for boys and University places entirely so.

The Grammar School buildings as seen in 1864. No further extensions were added to those seen here.

The buildings of Kay's school in the Wylde must have been very meagre for they were rebuilt in 1787 at a cost of £1,330 and enlarged in 1863 for £2,000 utilising land given to the school by Lord Derby in 1859. The two large class-rooms housed what was said to be, in 1869, "one of the wealthiest grammar school foundations in Lancashire".

114

The academic potential was never fully realised as most of the boys left at the age of 14 or 15 to enter their family business or join themselves to some commercial interest in the town, also the exhibitions were quite inadequate to pay even a worth-while proportion of the expenses at Oxford or Cambridge. In 1901 there were 152 boys in the school with eight masters and a Head all crammed into the Wylde school buildings.

Throughout its history there has been a bond between the Grammar School and the Church in Bury, although it is perhaps less evident today than in former years. The proximity of the school and the Church, before 1903, necessitated good-will by both the spiritual and academic leaders of the town. The Annual Vestry Meeting still has the right to appoint each year one of the Governors and it has been customary to elect the Rector, who for many years also served as Chairman. A further link were the grants paid by the Church to its Choir-boys for services rendered. Before World War II up to 50% of the school fees were offered by the Church to the boys in return for their weekly duties on Sunday, at least two choir practices and one mid-week Service. In this way the Grammar School also served as the Choir School for the town, sadly a practice which has died and which the Church today could ill afford.

The High School for Girls, Bolton Street, circa 1895
By kind permission of Borough Librarian.

In January, 1884, a completely independent Girls' School was opened in a house on Bolton Street opposite the Station. There were 23 girls on the first day to fill the three classes under the Headship of Miss Penelope Jane Kitchener. This High School for Girls was run as

The two classrooms which housed the Grammar School until 1901

a private company financed by a group of businessmen realising the need to educate the "fairer sex". The private endowment had a short life for in 1900 the school was handed over to the Governors of Bury Grammar School, whilst continuing in the Bolton Street premises. In 1903 the Boys' School left the Wylde for the more spacious accommodation in Tenterden Street which had been built at a cost of £45,000 and in 1906 the Girls' School, which numbered nearly 200 pupils, occupied the other half of the same building. Miss Kitchener remained Headmistress until her retirement in 1919. Although the two schools were under the same Board of Governors and within the same building for sixty years they remained two separate establishments and the only co-education was a sixth-form biology lesson for those specialising in the Medical World between the Wars. The Central Hall served both schools but time-tables were so designed that ne'er the twain should meet and the boys and girls used it quite independently. Since 1966 the Boys' Grammar School has been housed in new buildings erected on the one-time "first-eleven" football pitch and today the two schools cater for about 1,500 children, designated as a Direct Grant School by the Education Act of 1944.

The Church School

The glamour of education has shone from the Grammar School but it is another school which has done most to provide education for the succeeding generations of Bury people. In 1748 the Hon. and Rev. John Stanley founded a school for poor children and gave the incentive of providing clothing for its pupils if they would stay at school for at least eighteen months — a year was considered quite adequate in those days to acquire the necessary rudiments of knowledge. This outspoken Rector once said, in a Sermon, that his Parishioners were ". . . . the most cheating, pilfering, lying set of people I ever knew" and one reason for the violence, profaneness and irreligion in the town was "a want of education". Where the older grammar school had provided for a small handful of privileged children, Stanley's school catered for a much larger number of eighty boys and thirty girls. It is not known where this school was established but in 1772 £500 was collected and invested to buy land for a new school. During his lifetime the "Rev. John" gave, officially, three donations of £100 each to the school, which reflected the value he placed on education. The only known school master of the first school was a Daniel Nield who took up his work in the Charity School at the age of 65 and was finally buried, after eighteen years' teaching from 1775-1793, in St. John's Churchyard.

The present buildings in Haslam Brow are on the third known site on which the school has stood. The first known location was on the Rock, near the junction with Rochdale Road, the land being given by the Earl of Derby to erect a three-storey school and a school-master's house at the cost of £1,000. This "Free School" was opened in 1815 and within twenty years had grown to cater for 280 children. The teaching staff was just one Master and one Mistress, who must have had quite large classes !

The 1815 "Free School" on the corner of Clough Street and The Rock

The accommodation of the Free School was obviously taxed beyond stretching point and so in 1836 an overflow school was opened at Tenters Croft by the Rev. Geoffrey Hornby. This school, called the Irwell School, was for both sexes and "nothing contrary to virtue, good morals, or the doctrines of Christianity expounded by the Church of England should be taught". By 1871 this new school was as over-crowded as its mother school in the Rock, coping with 75 boys in a class-room little bigger than a normal house lounge. Compulsory education was enacted by Parliament in 1876 and one shudders to think how the children from the factories and mills crowded into the available space.

In 1887 the Irwell School and the Free School, now called the Central National School, moved their home to a new building at the corner of Lower Bank Street and Irwell Street, under the Headship of Mr. Thomas Gornall. In September, 1891, the school was made a free school to comply with the new Education Act and in the same year Mr. Gornall retired ". . . . after forty years' service in this school and the Central National School, Stanley Street". So ended an era of teaching whilst the work continued in the "1887" school buildings until 1964. The life and times of the school are recorded in the log books, in the Headmaster's keeping, and have been well presented in a thesis written by Mrs. C. Holt, a teacher of the school ; (a fascinating study which will perhaps one day be printed as a testimony to the years at the end of the last century). The school still continues as a Church of England school in the buildings opened in 1964.

118

Two schools with long and fine traditions of which Bury can be justly proud. It has been their task to educate the rising generations and their success, or failure, reflects itself in the community life. Over the past 150 years many other schools have come into being and in no way is their contribution belittled. The upsurge of the Lancashire Sunday School movement is an episode in itself as volunteers sought to provide an education service on the one day in the week when the operative could escape from the mills. Even though method and opportunity may alter, that standard of virtue, morals and Godliness which past generations deemed all important must ever remain of greater significance than academic achievement for which so many in our day alone crave.

The Central National School of 1887.

Photo : By courtesy of the Headmaster.

Interior of one of the classrooms. Notice the moveable partitions and heavy desks typical of their day.

CHAPTER 14—THE SECOND AND THIRD GENERATIONS

Bury's chimneys from the East.

The grey industrial scene viewed from the hills overlooking Bury is punctuated by the protruding sentinel-like factory chimneys. Each one looks very similar to its neighbour although a closer inspection will reveal some distinctive feature. The multitude of mills may look identical, yet within their walls can be found a host of different industries. Obviously the cotton industry has its place, having moved from the valleys ; then there is the water consuming industry of paper-making with its allied trades : calico-printing : forging and engineering. The people who built these mills and factories were a fascinating generation, but it was the second and third generations who enjoyed the prosperity.

Paper

Paper, hand-made or machine-made : paper for writing, printing and wrapping has found a place amongst Bury's foremost industries. James Wrigley & Son Ltd. became renowned across the world for their products. The founder took over Bridge Hall and its associated works in 1813 and added machine-made papers to the hand-making which was an established trade. Mr. Thomas Wrigley was the second generation and it was his rigorous regime that brought prosperity and fame par excellence to the firm. Its products varied from blotting-paper to white ivory boards for high class work and the firm had a regular order for newsprint with "The Times". Wrigley's continued as a family enterprise until the third generation when, in 1884, it was made into a private limited company. "Mr. Thomas" was a man of exceptional ability which was recognised in 1870 when he was appointed High Sheriff of the County of Lancaster. Amongst his many interests was

121

Mr. Thomas Wrigley: High Sheriff of the County of Lancaster.

his patronage of the arts. On his death in 1880 he left, besides a thriving paper-works, a fine art collection of oil and water paintings, engravings, plaques and sculpture which was later presented by his three sons to the town and can be seen in the Art Gallery which was especially erected to house this valuable collection. In the early 1920's the Company went into liquidation and the premises were finally acquired by Transparent Papers Ltd. in 1928.

The Entrance Portico of Bury's Art Gallery

Across the River Roach, facing Bridge Hall Mills, are the works of Yates Duxbury. The founder who gave his name to the firm was one-time manager for Heywood Higginbottom Ltd. at Bredbury. After succeeding with his son, Andrew, in a small way from 1863 at Hall-i'th'-Wood, Bolton, they bought the Heap Bridge Mill in 1882 and

"Annie". One of Yates Duxbury's locomotives, 0-4-0 built by Peckett and Sons: Bristol, 1908.

ran the two undertakings at the same time.   It is believed the Duxburys' new acquisition was then about 100 years old and stood ". . . . on the site of one of the earliest paper mills in Lancashire, known to have been in use in 1721".   Andrew's attempts to run a business were abysmal and he was replaced as a partner with his father by his youngest brother, Roger.   It was the youngest of the Duxburys who ultimately concentrated the work at Heap Bridge once he had sole charge and in 1908 built an entirely new mill which is an addition to the existing premises.

Felts

Yates Duxbury was not the only manager to start his own venture with good success. Beginning in 1838 three Porritt brothers had built a felt manufacturing empire including a mill at Helmshore. Their Manager at Helmshore was a Mr. J. H. Spencer who knew the felt process from A to Z.   In 1904 Mr. Spencer was sent to "Wrigley's" to consider a complaint from the famous client.   On his way to the appointment at Bridge Hall he spotted the empty Mossfield Mill of Hoyle & Sons, who had produced flannel for carding, and bought it.   It was by no means easy to start a new venture amidst the cut and thrust of the business world and it is known that on occasions Mr. Spencer had to sell some of the early machinery for scrap to raise the employees' wages. The obstacles were mastered and Spencer's was the first Bury firm to become "Round felt manufacturers". These continuous felts were made on a 34 foot long German machine especially imported in 1912.

Mossfield Mill

Mr. Spencer was a member of the Methodist Society and his family name appears on the foundation stones of the new Moulding Methodist Church. The strength of these Managers-turned-owners was that they were one with their workers and I have been told that going to work at Mossfield Mill was like going from "home to home". Mr. Spencer died in 1912 from a contagious disease which he picked up from wool in the mill and was buried at Park Congregational Chapel, the cortege walking from the tram terminus at Walmersley. By a strange twist of events which seem stranger than fiction, in 1914 the second generation of Spencer (three sons, Billy, Rowland and Horace and three daughters) amalgamated with the Helmshore felt manufacturers of Porritts and traded under the name of Porritts & Spencer Ltd. In 1968 the firm combined with a Blackburn based Company to create a sufficiently sized unit to exist in the high productivity world of the 1970's.

Another manufacturer of paper-makers' felts is James Kenyon and Sons Ltd. which celebrated its tri-centenary in 1964 and is reputed to be one of the oldest firms in the country. To celebrate the Anniversary Augustus Muir wrote "The Kenyon Tradition" and it would be presumptuous to try and emulate the work in the confines of this publication. James Kenyon first came to Bury from Crimble, near Heywood in 1827 and began to make woollen goods at Clerke Street. In 1841 he moved into the premises of John Young, a woollen manufacturer, which had been leased from the Rector in 1833; further land was acquired for expansion in 1867 and 1873.

For many years the Kenyon family lived at Walshaw Hall which was built in 1844 on the site of a previous house on the fringe of the little village. One of the earlier families to live at Walshaw was called Baron whose first known member was a Titus Baron, Churchwarden of Bury

The bridge over Derby Street linking two buildings of James Kenyon and Sons Ltd.

Parish Church for the township of Tottington during the year of the Restoration of the Monarchy 1662-63. The new hall was built in typical Victorian style by a Robert Whitehead from whom it was bought by Mr. James Kenyon in 1876 when he married the sister of his firm's Russian representative, Elsie Genth.

Sir Robert

Prestige is sought by the "old firm" club and a likely contender for membership is Peel Mills which had their early beginnings with the family of Sir Robert Peel, once Prime Minister of England. A Robert Peel is reputed to have been a manufacturer of woollen cloth in Blackburn in 1640 but it was "Grand-father Peel" who first brought the name to Bury in 1722 and rose to position of senior partner in the firm of calico-printers called Peel, Yates & Co. In 1783 "Father Peel" married the daughter of his partner and their third child and first son was the illustrious "Bobby" who was born in 1788 at their home Chamber Hall and was subsequently baptised in the Parish Church. In 1790 "Father Robert" built mills at Tamworth in Staffordshire and two years later entered Parliament as member for that borough. So successful were his business enterprises that he added £10,000 to the Government's appeal for funds to finance the Napoleonic Wars. Robert Peel the younger was educated at Harrow and Christ Church, Oxford, and entered Parliament, a born Tory, in 1809 by obtaining the seat of the Irish city Cashel but after the Reform Act of 1833 he became Member for his father's old constituency. In the post of Home Secretary, Peel reorganised the London Police Force and is perhaps better remembered for the "Bobbies" which sprang from the Metropolitan Police Act in 1830 than for either of his terms as Prime Minister (1834-1835 : 1841-1846) even though he did impose an outrageous income tax of 7d. in the £1 for three years. Sir Robert died in 1850 four days after being thrown from a horse in Hyde Park, a tragic end to a fine career. It would appear that Bury laid more claim to Peel than the family did to their home-town for after the death of his mother, the family seemed to lose interest in the Bury works and they concentrated their energies into their Midland factories.

126

Chamber Hall

Peel's home of Chamber Hall was owned at one time by the Green-halghs of Brandlesholme for a Miss Jane was married from the house in 1644. Its foundation was in Tudor times as a roof timber was found dated 1611. It was rebuilt in the 18th century and from 1866-1874 served as a Theological College of the Baptist Evangelical Union. Finally it was demolished in February, 1909.

The Grants

One of Peel's business ventures was in Ramsbottom where Father Robert had a mill in which was allocated a room for a Sunday School, the first in the town. Today Sunday Schools are mostly aimed at religious instruction to children but in the 19th century it was the sole opportunity many adults had to learn to read and write. Peel's interest at Ramsbottom was relatively short-lived for in 1806 William Grant, a Scottish farmer and his family left their home farm after a series of bad harvests to seek their fortunes elsewhere. They knew something of the prospects in Lancashire but he failed to obtain a suitable position even with a letter of introduction. Mr. Grant and his sons settled in Rams-bottom and legend has it that the tower, once a landmark overlooking the Irwell Valley, was built on the site where "a stick was put up, and where that fell, in that direction would they betake themselves for a house". ("Itinerary of Lancashire"). William Grant bought Sir Robert Peel's calico-printing mill and in 1812 added the cotton mill in Nuttall to his firm. To compete with his rivals he was able to sell his goods cheaper for the customer by having his own shop in The Rock, Bury. The story of the Grants is told by W. Hulme Elliot in his book

Nuttall Hall.   The home of the Grants, near Ramsbottom.

The Ship Inn, Bury Bridge.   The Magistrates' Court before the appointment of Mr. Grant.

"Country and Church of the Cheeryble Brothers" and at the time of writing the present Vicar of St. Andrew's, Ramsbottom, is preparing a more detailed account of the development of the town from the site of a tannery, a corn mill and numerous rookeries to the prosperity later enjoyed by the inhabitants.

Taken over by marriage

A close neighbour to the Peels of Blackburn was John Robinson Kay who was born in Burnley. In 1829, at the age of 24, John Robinson came, with his father to "the land of promise" on the banks of the Irwell at Summerseat and utilised its waters for mill-power. He was a man who wielded considerable influence in his generation and became a Director of the Lancashire and Yorkshire Railway (which may account for the fine railway viaduct adjacent to Brooksbottoms Mill, Summerseat), he also had interest in banking, insurance and was prominent in the Old Wesleyan Methodist Society.

Another early cotton enterprise was established at Bacup by Joshua Hoyle in 1834. Joshua had two sons, Isaac and Edward and it was the elder who married the daughter of John Robinson and Mary Kay. When Isaac's father-in-law died in 1872 Brooksbottoms was added to the Joshua Hoyle & Sons combine which included three mills in Bacup, one in Shawforth and a fine warehouse in Manchester. The firm of Joshua Hoyle & Sons Ltd. has continued to use the motto created by its founder "No test, like time", which reveals something of the pride and confidence the past generations had in their products.

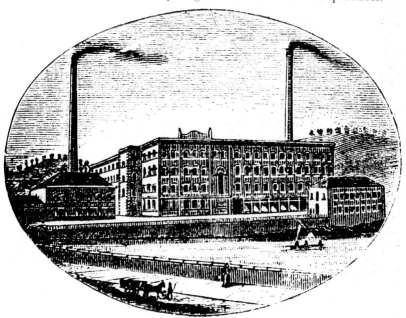

Brooksbottom Mill, Summerseat, circa 1890.

The Entrance Portico, Robinson Kay Home

The common factor

The link between the industries of Bury was that they all required machinery following the Industrial Revolution period, and firms were justly proud of their steam engines. In a Directory of Lancashire Industries published towards the end of the last century the entry of Jas. R. Crompton & Bros. Ltd., Elton Paper Works, includes a list of twelve engines and their builders. One of these was built by William Kay of the Phoenix Foundry, Bury, and was rated at 24 horse-power. The design drawing of the engine shows that the flywheel was nearly 15 feet in diameter — a fact to remember when viewing the greatly reduced reproduction of the elevation and it is difficult to realise that a man could comfortably walk between the columns. Another supplier of engines to Crompton's is named as Chas. Walmsley, Atlas Iron Works, Elton, which has grown in its one hundred years life to the mighty combine of today.

A firm which supplied Kay with his basic material was that of Joseph Webb's, founded in 1846. Joseph originated in the Staffordshire "black country" and established his works as a rolling mill for

130

The staircase, Robinson Kay Home

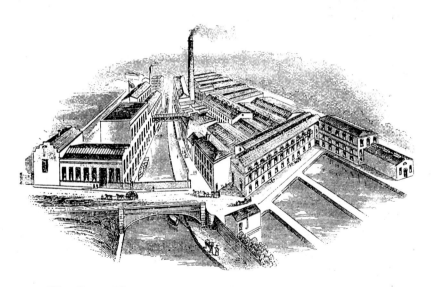

Elton Paper Works, spanning the Bury-Bolton-Manchester Canal.

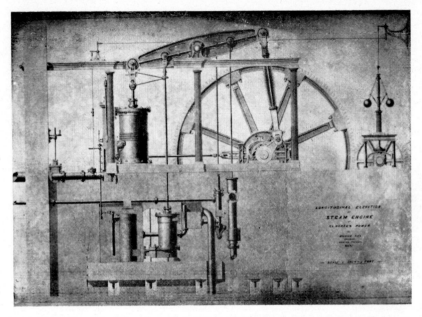

A reduced reproduction of scale drawing of Steam Engine, rated at 24 horse-power by William Kay for Jas. R. Crompton.

bars used in textile machinery on a spur of the canal which extended under the road at Bury Bridge. For many first generation industrialists there was no fine house or Victorian stately home and Joseph, with his family, lived in the building which he first built as the rolling mill and has now been converted into offices. Later he added a forge in which he was able to produce the high degree of work and finish necessary for the centre shafts of the steam engines. Joseph Webb had two sons, Henry and George, who joined their father in his firm and a member of the fourth generation is today one of the directors. At the turn of the century the firm expanded to include constructional engineering but over more recent years it has had to specialise in its work. The family concern lost its individual identity when it was taken over by William Parks of Wigan and it was the new parent company which dismantled and moved the forge to Wigan leaving only the machine shop and constructional engineering plant in Bury.

We shall overcome

The main industries of Bury are symbolised in the Coat of Arms granted on 28th February, 1877, by Garter Principal King of Arms, Clarence King of Arms and Norroy King of Arms. In the quarters are four representations : the Anvil for the forging : the golden fleece for wool : a pair of crossed shuttles for the cotton industry and a papyrus plant for the paper trade. Above is a closed visor capped by a bee which is supported by the cotton plant. Its Motto "Vincit omnia Industria" means "Industry overcomes all things".

132

Bury Coat of Arms

Many of the men who founded and developed the industries in Bury were most industrious but turned their backs on the Motto and were sincere and sound Christian men of faith. Some of the conditions which their emplyees endured may seem to us far from right yet their practice of religion in regular worship, sponsoring of Churches and Chapels and Sunday Schools speak of a testimony of concern. The times were often hard, the pressures of work overpowering amidst ruthless competition but a large measure of their success was due to living out in public what they believed in their hearts and the life we now enjoy is the fruit of their endeavours to improve the lot of their fellow men.

CHAPTER 15—ALONG THE ROACH

The valley of the Roach between Transparent Papers (right) and Yates Duxbury's.

Just as the River Irwell had attracted families to settle by its banks so the Roach had a similar appeal. The Holts of Bridge Hall and the Heywoods of Heywood Hall were two of the early settlers to claim a parcel of land in the overgrown tract of country bordering the river in the area known as Heap, a name thought to be corrupted from the Saxon word "Heep" meaning a mass of irregularities. Even before they arrived the Romans had marched across the land leaving a small clay urn containing coins dating to about A.D. 268 in the reign of Claudius II. This was found when certain alterations were being made at Plumpton Hall, near Hooley Bridge during the last century.

Bridge Hall

Travelling east from Bury, Bridge Hall is the first ancient family residence you pass. The earliest reference to its existence is in 1445 when a "John Holt of the Bridge" is mentioned. One hundred and fifty years later Roger Holt died on 5th September, 1594, holding the estate ". . . . called Bridge Hall, a water mill adjoining . . . of the

Earl of Derby . . . . by a rent of 2s. 0d. per annum". One of Roger's sons, Peter, helped to defend Bolton against the attack of the Derbys' during the Civil War and earned the nickname "Captain Holt". Althougu the Earl of Derby lost his head in Bolton, the Holts escaped unscathed at the Restoration and remained in occupation of Bridge Hall until it was sold to a cousin by a family "consortium". Love built bridges across the gulf of the Civil War for Roger Holt, a Parliamentarian, married Jane Greenhalgh of Chamber Hall in 1644.

Heywood literally means "a fenced area of a wood". Hey meaning a hedge or fence. The land with "appurtenances and easements" was granted by Adam de Bury to Peter of Heywood in about 1286 for a yearly payment of 2s. 0d. per annum to be paid on the feast of King Oswald (August 5th). During the Civil War the Heywood family mortgaged the estate to John Starky of Rochdale to raise money to help the Royalists and in 1717 they sold their interests outright. One of the many Peters in the Heywood family was a Westminster magistrate who helped to frustrate Guy Fawkes' attempt to blow-up Parliament, and in 1640, was himself stabbed to death in Westminster Hall by a Dominican Friar for his Protestant loyalty. His epitaph in St. Anne's, Aldergate Street, London, says "Reader ! if not a Papist bred, Upon such ashes lightly tread". Another Peter was a midshipman in the famous mutiny on the Bounty in 1789.

The 1640 Chapel at Heywood

In the seventeenth century the Heywood's home was rebuilt, the Hall in 1611 and the Chapel in 1640. Due to the unrest in the 1640's the Chapel was never consecrated and became a strong-hold of the Puritans under the patronage of Robert Heywood. His heir, however, was akin to the Vicar of Bray first holding a commission in Cromwell's army and later becoming a devoted friend of the 7th Earl of Derby. In 1805 the Chapel was enlarged to meet the growing population of Heywood and was finally replaced by the present St. Luke's in 1859. "The old building was in itself a disgrace to any Christian community. It is impossible to give by description in words a just idea of its mean and most wretched appearance. In one place in the galleries (which surrounded three sides of the building), a tall man could almost touch the ceiling with his head ; the building was oppressively close, and highly offensive, there was not so much as a font, for which a most unbecoming substitute had been provided" — (The Church Builder : April, 1862).

Kenyon's Crimble Mill

It has been said "The history of Heywood is the history of cotton" and the phrase does sum up the happenings on the banks of the Roach. In 1714 Edward Kenyon began the manufacture of woollen goods at Crimble and from that time the town grew and expanded, firstly along the edge of the Roach and its fast flowing tributaries such, as the Chees-den and Naden Brooks, but later round the canal terminal and railway station. Prosperity increased with industry and even minor recessions brought poverty and hardship to the people.

One of the most influential families in Heywood was the Fenton's of Crimble. As early as 1754 a John Fenton was Church-warden of St. Luke's Chapel and he centred a hand-woven flannel industry on a tombstone in the Churchyard — the place where he conducted the buying and selling of home-made cloth   The family gradually accum-ulated a large fortune by the wool and flannel trade and a certain Joseph Fenton was one of the original partners of a private bank called "Fenton, Eccles, Cunliffe and Roby". In Baines' "History of the County Palatine of Lancaster" of 1824 this is the only bank, besides the Savings Bank, which is listed to hold business in Bury. In 1814 Joseph

Fenton's Grave at Bamford Chapel

Left: The drive to Crimble Hall

built Crimble Hall for his eldest son John who successfully added to the family wealth by opening several cotton mills. At the 1833 election John was returned to Parliament as Liberal M.P. for Rochdale, the constituency he represented till 1841 when he resigned through ill-health. The Member lived for a further twenty-two years until he died at the age of 73 and was buried at Bamford Chapel. He was an active Christian man and we are told "If the weather was wet on the Sabbath he made it a practice to go to Bamford Chapel in his clogs, accompanied by his favourite dog, "Crib", who for years was not known to absent himself from his religious duties". (The Social and Political History of Rochdale by W. Robertson).

It was immediately before the 1860's cotton famine that the first real disaster hit Heywood with the failure of Fenton's cotton empire. In 1858 there was a bitter family squabble which ultimately led to the closing of their industrial concerns. Unfortunately it was only three years before the depression which began in 1861. The hardship lasted for six years as the American Civil War curtailed all shipments of cotton to England. Then the Fenton's private bank was forced into liquidation in 1878 with liabilities totalling £300,000 after the collapse of the Cornwall Railway Company in which the bank held large investments. Joseph, the third child of John Fenton, M.P. by his first wife, and at one time one of the wealthiest men in South-East Lancashire, had the awful experience of watching his possessions sold and estate bought by the highest bidder to pay the creditors. Unfortunately what monies were realised could not restore trade and confidence and many people left Heywood, whilst others, financially ruined, struggled to rebuild a new life.

138

Mutual Mills

In 1881 Heywood received its Charter of Incorporation as a borough and perhaps it is due to the faith of the first mayor, Mr. Isherwood, in his fellow townsfolk that Heywood was to rise from the Fenton ruin. The first mark of encouragement was the building of No. 1 Mutual Mill in 1884 which was followed seven years later by what was then the largest spinning mill under one roof in the world, the Yew Mill. In 1920 alterations began to take place as the Mutual Mill added man-made fibres to their schedule. Over a period of two hundred years the cotton industry had transformed Heywood from a hamlet-in-a-wood to a prosperous cotton town, but the story is incomplete; difficult times were still ahead.

From the end of World War I changes have been needed to meet the demands of the present and future. The inter-War years were days of depression for many parts of Lancashire and few suffered worse than Heywood. In 1934 the clouds were ominous as four spinning mills closed and by the end of 1938 another nine had shut their doors. The tally of closures from 1919 to 1939 was twenty-three spinning mills and three other manufacturers, of the ones still working the

The head of the branch canal to Heywood. The warehouse was built in 1871.

majority were only working half-time. Some mill-owners changed to the production of high quality towelling in an endeavour to avoid what seemed the inevitable final day. Heywood had gained a reputation for its towels through William R. Lee who had begun the industry in 1873. Many of the empty mills were demolished, including the Yew Mill, and at one period half the town's working population of 10,000 was unemployed and the Government classified it as a "depressed area". The cotton trade is now just one of the many industries and skills of the town. In 1963 only nine mills were open but new industries entered the area both before and after World War II and the pattern of life is no longer geared to the fluctuations of cotton.

Heywood is still a town of change, seeking to create new opportunities. In 1970 the canal branch was filled in and the one hundred years' old wharf warehouse stands towering up like the pelican in the desert, utilised as a storage warehouse. The railway station is scheduled to close and the future life-line will be the Lancashire-Yorkshire motorway which skirts the southern borders of the town.

Heywood Market Place today dominated by St. Luke's spire.

POSTSCRIPT

The prophet Isaiah told those who would seek the hand of God in their lives to "look to the rock from which you were hewn, to the quarry from which you were dug" (51 v. 1). In these pages I have tried to dig a spadeful here and another one there, sometimes perhaps a little too shallow. Many areas of life and geography have had, by necessity, to have had sparse attention, but I have tried to show something of the complex pattern made on God's weaving loom to produce the life of the ancient Parish of Bury. Into this changing scene came the first congregation of our Church : the first cotton operatives to the mill : the first Commissioner for the town : the first "Co-oper" at the shop. It is the threads of their lives and the countless others crossing each other and interweaving which have given us our story or, rather, God's story for us.

Looking down the centuries of history some words of Jeremiah sums up all that history both records and leaves vacant "Mine heritage is unto me as a speckled bird". The quarry from which we are dug contains very mixed material and is speckled with desires and endeavours of men and women for good or ill, for prosperity or selfish gain, for Godliness or evil. With all their faults I commend these pages in this age when tradition is frowned upon and certain forces would like to destroy all that is past to produce their own Utopia, but even revolutionaries must work in God's quarry.

The scene across the valleys and moors today is so very different from when the cotton operatives struggled up from Bircle Dene to take part in the Consecration of their Church on 1st July, 1846, yet they worshipped the same Heavenly Father in the same faith of the Lord Jesus Christ as the present congregation. The rock is of God's making : the quarry is of God's working.

> Look to the rock from which you were hewn,
> to the quarry from which you were dug.

141

BIBLIOGRAPHY

History, Directory and Gazetteer of the County Palatine of Lancaster : Vol. 1 by Edward Baines (1824).

An Itinerary of Lancashire (1844).

The History of Bury : *Lancashire.* 1660-1875 by Miss M. Gray (1965) Published by Bury Times (1970).

County Borough of Bury 1876-1926 *Jubilee Souvenir.*

History of the Borough of Bury by B. T. Barton (1874).

The Victoria History of the County of Lancaster (Vol. 5). Farrer and Brownhill (1911).

Notes on Holcombe by the Rev. H. Dowsett (1902).

Samuel Crompton : *Inventeur de metier a filer.* Dobson & Barlow Ltd. (1927).

The History of Park Congregational Church by the Rev. W. E. Harding (1931).

Memorials of Christian Church, Bury by Thos. H. Hayhurst (1910).

A Century of Methodism in Bury by Thos. H. Hayhurst (1890).

History of Brunswick Church, Bury by T. P. Dale (1896).

Minutes of Lancashire and Yorkshire Railway and East Lancashire Railway.

Directory of Lancashire Industries.

The Kenyon Tradition by Augustus Muir (1964).

Bury Parish Church : *Jubilee* 1876-1926. 'Senex'' (1925).

History of St. Luke's Church, Heywood by Canon G. V. H. Eliott (1962).

The Origin and the History of Co-operation in Bury by Thomas Rigby (1905).

Booklets published by the Transport Depts. of Bury and Ramsbottom (both 1969).

Centenary booklet of Bury Trustee Savings Bank (1922).

Bury Grammar School (Old Girls' Association) Jubilee Edition (1934).

ABOUT THE AUTHOR

The Rev. Arthur J. Dobb was born at Fairfield, Droylsden and received his secondary education at Audenshaw Grammar School. At the age of sixteen he entered the Regional College of Art, Manchester and successfully completed the five-year course in Architecture gaining the Diploma of Associateship of the College and subsequently the Associateship of the Royal Institute of British Architects. After four years practising as an Architect, during which time he qualified as a Lay Reader in the Diocese of Southwark, he commenced training for the Ministry at Oak Hill Theological College. After the two-year course he was ordained by the Bishop of Manchester in 1958 to serve a curacy at St. Paul's, Deansgate, Bolton with the Rev. Canon R. C. Craston and a second curacy at St. Mary's, Rawtenstall under the Vicar and Rural Dean of Rossendale, the Rev. H. K. Turner. In 1962 he was appointed Vicar of St. John the Baptist, Bircle.

His wife, Kathleen, has been a lifelong friend as they attended the same elementary day school and grew up in the same Church Fellowship at St. Clement's, Higher Openshaw. Prior to their marriage in September, 1960 Mrs. Dobb was Secretary to the Fairfield High School for Girls. They have five children : from left to right, David, Julie, Joanne, Katina and Philip.

Printed by
BURY TIMES LIMITED
Cross Street, Bury